DECODING EZEKIEL'S TEMPLE

J.M.Allen

Decoding Ezekiel's Temple

© J.M.Allen 1999 with Appendix A, May 2010

© 2014

Author's edition

Printed by CreateSpace, an Amazon.com company

ISBN-13: 978-1505314670

J.M.Allen,
Cambridge
England

CONTENTS

3

Books by J.M. Allen

Atlantis: The Andes Solution
The Atlantis Trail
Atlantis: Lost Kingdom of the Andes
Atlantis and the Persian Empire
Tiwanaku: A City Lost in Time
Decoding the Tiwanaku Calendar
The Easiread System of Musical Notation
for Piano and Keyboards

Decoding Ezekiel's Temple
Who surveyed the Earth in the Remote Past?

Introduction

WHEN WE THINK of ancient civilisations, images spring to mind of great stone pyramids in Egypt, stepped ziggurats in Mesopotamia and sacrificial temples in Aztec Mexico where countless victims were thrown to their deaths in honour of some presently forgotten god.

We are readily impressed by such stone monuments whether it be Cheops' Great Pyramid itself, or its similarly sized counterpart in Mexico, or a simple arrangement of massive stones into a circle such as that at Stonehenge on Salisbury Plain in England.

But what is more impressive is, or ought to be, the thought processes that went into the constructing of these features. What were the builders looking for? What did they hope to achieve, particularly in the case of the stone rings? Do we really understand their function? And is not the intellectual effort of their conception greater by far than the physical effort of their construction?

Our forebears have been around in a form similar to us for many thousands of years. Was their intellect in any way inferior to ours?

Go and gaze upon the ruins of the city of Tiahuanaco on the Bolivian Altiplano and the guide will point out a giant stone statue representing one of the thinkers of this mysterious ancient civilisation. "Look at the ankles" he will say. "Observe how they have been deliberately broken. That is because these were the intellectuals, forbidden to do any manual work and their ankles subsequently smashed to prevent them running away and to concentrate their minds on the tasks in hand."

It is thought by some that a world wide energy grid once covered the Earth, whose residential energy traces are to be detected along what are called 'ley' lines connecting religious and other significant sites, also that stone circles fulfilled some mysterious function such as gateways to time travel.

Prof Alexander Thom detected a standard unit of length in the stone circles of the British Isles which he called a 'megalithic yard' and defined as a unit of 2.72ft or to be more precise, 2.7199 English feet which is 32.64″

It may be a surprise to some to discover that their ancestors, previously thought of as primitive 'stone age' beings should bother with a standard unit of measurement.

What is a greater surprise is that this megalithic yard represents the distance travelled by the planet Earth on its orbit in a 36,000th part of a second!

This is no mere coincidence, because the Sumerian standard unit of 33.0″ is also the distance the Earth would travel in a 36,000th of a second if we were to use a purely mathematical year of 360 days and don't forget the number 360 or 360 x 100 = 36000 was the key to Babylonian or Sumerian mathematics.

But the megalithic yard of the stone circles has a yet more interesting defining equation as to its length, namely by using the constants of speed of light x ∏ divided by the length of the solar year, which anyone with a calculator can verify gives a unit of 2.7199ft – exactly the length to four decimal places which Prof Thom specifies for the length of the megalithic yard in the appendix to his "Megalithic Sites in Britain".

So were the stone rings portals of time travel to other dimensions? Who knows. Did they wait for a specific day when the Earth's distance from the sun was in harmony with the numerical constant for the speed of light? Who knows.

The Earth's distance from the sun gives our planet the unique climatic ranges essential for man's survival. Could an advanced intelligence fix that distance to give us the beneficial range we require, and fix the length of the year accordingly?

Consider this. The length of the solar year in seconds equals a 100th of the equatorial circumference of the Earth in half-inches.

A coincidence? Or did someone fix the length of the year as the signature of his handiwork? And why half-inches? - Because the most logical unit of measurement derived from the dimensions of the planet Earth which we live upon, would be to take the polar diameter of the planet and divide by 1,000,000,000 – which gives a unit of half an inch - (put another way, it is actually the inch which is a double unit.)

And it has already been done before since details are given in Ezekiel's description of the Holy Temple where decimal and duodecimal multiples of the half-inch are used as the basis for the previously unidentified 'great' and 'sacred' cubits used to measure the Temple. Confirmation of these units is again given in the Revelation of St John where a mysterious city in the form of a giant cube 1.42 statute miles long on each side is seen "descending out of heaven".

A cube? A city? A space city? A time-travelling city? The 'angel' who measured it carried a golden reed to measure the city, which was identical to that measured for Ezekiel, and the measurements were given to Man. That these units of measurement should be precisely derived from the diameter of the planet in such ancient times is astounding.

Does Ezekiel's description of the Heavenly City contain some mysterious key to time-travel? Did some superior being fix the planet on its orbit and give a spur to mankind? At the very least it begs the question – Who surveyed the Earth in the remote past?

Chapter 1

Crystalline Earth

THE POWER of the atom is its ability to sustain a chain reaction. This book began with a reaction, in as much as one thought provokes another, and it is hoped that the material within its pages may provoke a similar reaction within the reader.

It may surprise the reader to learn that the English Inch is derived from the decimal division of the Earth's polar diameter and that the ancient Egyptian foot of 300mm is derived from the division of the circumference of the planet.

It almost begs the question – who surveyed the Earth in the remote past? And was there ever a global grid connecting points of energy resulting in centres which can still be traced as ley lines today?

But before one can embark on a study of grids involving maps, charts and distances, we have to consider the units we are going to use and this in turn leads to a study of all our present linear units of measurement as well as the mysterious 'cubits' of the past.

Today, we have three choices open to us when measuring distances on a modern map. Using the metric system, we would use kilometres. Navigators, travelling over the surface of the globe would probably prefer to use nautical or geographic miles. The kilometre and the geographic mile have similar origins in that they are both derived from a division of the Earth's circumference. In ancient times the circumference of the Earth was divided into 360 degrees comprising four quadrants each of 90 degrees. Each degree in turn was divided into 60 geographic miles which was further subdivided into 6,000 geographic feet. The geographic mile is the length of a minute of latitude, taken today as 6076.8884ft and 'rounded up' by the British Admiralty to 6080ft. In antiquity the calculation was much simpler, since the geographic mile was by definition 6,000ft and the length of the geographic foot was correspondingly larger than the English foot of 12" having an average length of 308mm or 12.125".

The Metric system in use today was introduced in 1795 by the French revolutionaries with the following objectives;

(a)   The spirit of the revolution called for a man-made measure to replace the former 'Divine' units.

(b)   There was a need for a single measurement unit to replace the numerous different and confusing types then in use.

(c)   The new unit was to be decimal for simplicity and was required to relate to the dimensions of the Earth.

To meet these requirements, the French divided the circumference of the Earth into four quadrants and each quadrant not into degrees or miles but into 10,000,000 new units which they called metres.

The third possible unit of measurement is the English Statute Mile, comprising 5280 feet, 1760 yards or 63,360 inches. The English units of feet and inches have been much derided and most people were taught at school that feet yards and inches were derived from parts of the body belonging to some obscure king; but this is really not so. The origin of the English foot will be demonstrated later, and it may surprise the reader to learn that the English foot and the Geographic foot are derived respectively from the diameter and the circumference of the Earth; in support of the latter statement, the reader may like to consider the following.

In the year 1750, James Stuart and Nicholas Revett set out for Greece to measure the front of the Parthenon. The scholars of their time were deeply interested to learn the exact length of the Greek foot, since it was reported that the Greek foot was computed as the 1/6000th part of a minute of latitude, and from the length of a minute of latitude, they could compute the size of the Earth.

The Parthenon was built in 438BC on the orders of Pericles, to replace the former Temple of Athena which had been burnt down in the Persian Wars. It was nicknamed by the Greeks Hecatompedon, for its front was intended to measure 100 Greek feet. The length of the temple was intended as 150 Greek cubits and the interior accordingly, 10,000 square Greek cubits.

So, armed with specially prepared measuring equipment, Stuart and Revett measured the front of the Parthenon and found it to be 101.141 English feet (30.828 metres), which meant that each Greek foot had a length of 12.136" or 308.277mm. This in turn gives a minute of latitude of 6068.46 feet which is the length of a minute of latitude on the Greek parallel of 37°40'N, the parallel of Olympia.

From the centrifugal force inherent in a spinning body, Sir Isaac Newton deduced that the Earth bulged at the equator and was flattened at the poles. This means that the Earth is not a perfect sphere and that when we talk of the Earth's circumference, we have to remember that the Earth's equatorial circumference (24,902.442 st.miles from the International Spheroid) is larger than the Earth's polar circumference (24,818.078 st.miles from the British Astronomical Association Handbook) and a minute of latitude has a diminishing value from the equator (6046.3418ft) right up to the pole (6107.7755ft).

This is why a Greek foot had a slightly different value to an Egyptian foot, since the length of their geographic foot depended on the latitude of their observatory.

The importance of this fact is that if we find an ancient building in some forgotten corner of the world and find it to be built in feet of a certain dimension, then by studying the length of the unit of construction and the mathematical system of measurement, we can try and establish the origins of the builder.

By way of illustration, suppose many years from now, a space vehicle from a distant galaxy enters the Solar system to land on the planet Mars in search of life there. The two occupants set foot on the landscape and cast around for signs of occupation.

Near the ship they find scorch marks on the rocky ground, together with a peculiar arrangement of shallow indentations. One of them picks up an artefact. A cylindrical metal container, pierced at one end. They take it back to the ship for analysis and find that the diameter of the container is exactly five of their own measuring units, a coincidence. The younger team member feeds the data into the computer and finds that this dimension is exactly a 100,000,000th part of the radius of one of the planets in the group – not the planet on which they have landed, but the next one towards the sun.

The Senior dismissed this as a coincidence since that planet is known to have been dead for hundreds of years, and the atmosphere still hideously contaminated by lethal radiation. Still, he labels the artefact with the data and the position where found and files it away, another exhibit for the museum back home, though he ponders all the while about the mysterious characters on the side..... COKE.

It was hoped that the splitting of the atom would herald a new era of cheap energy for mankind. Einstein's famous equation $e=mc^2$ where e = energy, m = matter and c = the speed of light, demonstrated that energy and matter are equivalent. When matter is destroyed or converted into energy, the energy released in the accompanying nuclear reactions is of tremendous proportions.

A conventional power plant burns large quantities of coal, oil or gas to produce heat. This is used to produce steam, which drives a turbo generator. In the nuclear power plant, only a comparatively small quantity of fuel is needed. The heat generated in the process is carried away by the coolant and electricity generated as before.

The unit cost of electricity in the early years of nuclear power has been higher than that generated conventionally but it has been hoped that costs would fall as technology advanced. But the limited supplies of fossil fuels and the great demand for electricity by the industrial nations has encouraged the development of nuclear power, although sometimes in the face of opposition from those parties who point out the attendant dangers of the nuclear programme.

The energy potential latent in the atom was publicly demonstrated in 1945 when the first atomic bomb was dropped on Japan. This is the irony of nuclear energy, that although its benefits are considerable when peacefully applied, it can also be developed to produce weapons of mass destruction, so terrifying that for a time the very fear of their power prevents them from being used.

When the nuclear device is exploded, an uncontrolled chain reaction takes place. In the power station, the reaction is controlled, the fuel rods being interspaced with control rods which can regulate the rate of the reaction or extinguish it completely. The release of the energy is accompanied by radioactivity so the plant has to incorporate protective shields to contain this dangerous by-product. The fuel rods are handled by remote control, the spent elements are usually reprocessed at another site to recover any unused fuel and are eventually encased in concrete to be dumped at sea. The accompanying radioactivity is one of the main objections to the use of nuclear power in that no entirely satisfactory method has been put forward to dispose of the spent elements, which will continue to decay for thousands of years, also the possibility that an accident may occur at a plant or fuel in transit, releasing radioactivity into the atmosphere.

If it were possible to harness some other form of energy, for example related to the Earth's magnetic field, it may be necessary to arrange the 'collectors' in a geometric pattern. Such a system could be similar to the ancient 'ley' lines which criss-cross the country. Some authors have considered that the standing stones, found all over the British Isles, because of their quartz crystalline nature may have been used to convey or pick up energy.

A crystalline pattern connecting many of the sites of antiquity was identified by Russian scientists a few years ago. They considered the surface of the Earth to be covered with 12 regular pentagons and twenty triangles. For reasons of magnetic anomalies they were said to influence the siting of ancient shrines and temples. The system was derived from the points of greatest magnetic disturbance, such as in the "Bermuda Triangle" where a number of ships and aircraft are said to have vanished under mysterious circumstances.

Because of its daily rotation on its axis, the Earth is essentially a dynamo and is surrounded by a very strong magnetosphere. As long as the Earth continues to turn, this potential energy will continue to be available, without the dangers adhering to nuclear fuels and without the threat to the environment caused by burning fossil fuels in large quantities. It may be left to future generations to find a method of harnessing this energy, but it may be that this occult power was known in antiquity.

With the present day equator most of the land surface of the globe lies in the northern hemisphere and the largest oceans in the southern hemisphere. An equator bisecting Europe would more evenly divide the globe, bearing in mind that the land of Antarctica is presently lost under ice.

A very advanced technical civilisation might possibly develop the ability to control a planet's orbit, speed and inclination, both to harness its energies and make the most use of the land area, as well as to enjoy the climatic benefits of being at an ideal distance from the sun.

Indeed, the north pole has not always been where it is today. For most of geological time, it lay over the part of the globe now occupied by the Pacific Ocean, but at that time the configuration of the land masses themselves was different. The continents we know today were originally one 'super continent' which gradually broke apart to become our modern continents after drifting across the surface of the globe. South America split off from Africa to become an island and eventually join up with North America which had split off from what is now Europe.

The axis of the Earth has always pointed to the same area in space, but the shell, 'floating' on a molten interior, has wandered over the axis and in almost recent times, the north pole was located in Hudson's Bay, about 30° from its present location. At that time North America would have been covered in ice with a cold climate extending almost to Mexico, while a warm climate would have prevailed in northern Siberia and parts of Antarctica.

Chapter 2

Falmouth's Little Pyramid

IT WAS purely by chance that I discovered "Falmouth's Little Pyramid". I had been heading in the direction of St Michael's Mount but owing to a shortage of time had decided to pay Falmouth a visit instead. I should have left the train at the normal halt which is more centrally placed for access to the town, but not being familiar with the area, remained on the train to the end of the line. This brought me to the far end of the town, close to Pendennis Castle and I set out to walk back to the town centre.

On my way into town I came across a curious monument – a stone pyramid. At first sight it seemed to be no more than the usual war memorial but strangely, it did not bear any inscription or plaque. Intrigued, I called in at the local photographic shop where there was an historic collection of picture postcards of the town to inquire more of the history of the pyramid and perhaps to obtain a postcard of it.

The shop owner showed me a collection of photos of clipper ships, fishing smacks and relicks of days gone by, but only one included the monument and it was too small to be of much use. I happened to ask if the monument had always been on that site or had perhaps been removed from some other location. To my surprise he replied that it had been put there some time back, having originally been at the top of the hill. In moving it he said, they had lost the original capstone and replaced it with one of a different colour. This was just like the Great Pyramid which had also lost its capstone over the years. I replied that the little pyramid was possibly the most important thing in the whole town and was further surprised when the shopkeeper answered that it could well be – the man who built the pyramid also built the town!

Further investigation at the local library revealed that the pyramid had been constructed on the instructions of Mr Martin Killigrew in 1737 and had originally stood where it stands today. It had been moved to the top of the hill, but had later been moved back on the instructions of a later member of the Killigrew family. The history of the pyramid had been found recorded in a bottle sealed up in the pyramid and exposed when it was moved for the second time.

The pyramid

..... "Old Falmouth"

"The following is a copy relating to the Killigrew monument written on parchment and sealed up in a bottle, and then built into the interior of the said monument (about half-way up), on its erection on Arwenack Green on the 18th July 1871, viz:

"The Killigrew Monument"

"This pyramid was originally built in the Grove near Arwenack, AD 1737-1738, from the design and at the cost of Mr Martin Killigrew, (son-in-law of the second and last Sir Peter Killigrew), who was some-time recorder of Falmouth and for several years steward of the Arwenack Estate. His original name was Lister; he was born in 1666 at Liston,

Staffordshire, and whilst a captain or lieutenant at Pendennis Castle, under John, Earl of Bath, he became acquainted with the Killigrews, and upon his marriage with Ann, Sir Peter's youngest daughter, he took the name of Killigrew. He survived all the members of the Arwenack family with the exception of the grand-nieces, - through the younger of whom, the present and first Earl of Kimberley inherits the Arwenack Estate. The object in the erection of this pyramid does not appear very clear unless (which is not improbable) it was intended as a family monument of the Killigrews.

Mr Martin Killigrew in several letters to Mr Abraham Hall, the then steward of Arwenack, gave full instructions in detail as to the manner in which the pyramid was to be built, but said nothing of the object he had in its erection, except what is contained in the following extracts from his letters, viz:-

"St. James's, 29th March, 1737. Now again as to the pyramid, fearing I shall tire you with my tedious instructions in the case. But to proceed in such an affair as one ought requires previous thought and necessary provision," etc… "Without having my foolish vanity exposed I may tell you, that in having this projection carried out into a just execution, as it ought and I hope will be, I pretend to insist that from the sheltered position and durableness of the Stone (manual violence excepted) the thing may stand a beauty to the Harbour without limitation of time, and you and your posterity have the honour of the Architecture. Should the workmen know my designe of painting it, they would depend

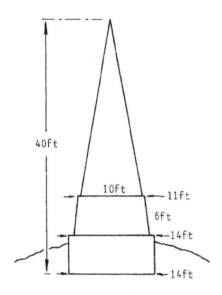

The Killigrew Monument

thereon for covering their defects by puttee and paint, which I would by all means avoid."

"St. James's, 9th Aprill, 1737. You must keep yourself in cash on my account; for ye enabling you readily at all times to pay (as you shall see reasonable) on account of this pyramid; a darling thing I am never to see, but shall have much pleasure thereby in living to ye being duly informed of its being raised and finished to perfection according to ye Modell and my directions," etc.

"St. James's. 16th May, 1737....I have already charged you in the most Special manner and must now repeat it, and shall rely on your care therin, that there be no inscription in or about the Pyramid or the whole grove, no, not so much as the date of the year, Hoping it may remain a beautiful Imbellishment to the harbour, Long, Long after my desiring to be forgatt, as if I had never been."

"Old Falmouth"...
"The entire height of the pyramid is forty feet, and its base fourteen feet square. It remained in the

Grove from the date of its erection there until 1836, when it was removed for the purpose of making room for the row of houses known as "Grove Place", - at the same time the grove of fine elm trees which formed avenues radiating in all directions from the Pyramid except towards the harbour was swept away. The Pyramid was then erected under the superintendence of Mr Josiah Devonshire, builder, near the top of the hill towards the bay, in which position however, it never showed to advantage. Since its erection on that site, the feature of the neighbourhood has altered entirely. The Cornwall Railway has been constructed close to its base, public docks have been formed only a short distance off, a carriage drive has been made around Pendennis Castle, and buildings have sprung up on every side. In carrying out the latter, the apparent height of the pyramid was considerably diminished, it became almost entirely hid, and obstructed the view from the houses in its immediate vicinity, more particularly those belonging to the house built by Captn. Saulez, RN (Landsdowne House), on the site of whose back garden it stood until June, 1871, when by order of the Right Honourable John, First Earl of Kimberley, it was removed to Arwenack Green in front of the old Manor House, where it now stands."

The intriguing thing about the Killigrew pyramid is that the architect, for what designs we know not, went to considerable trouble to ensure that the monument was built precisely as instructed at a time when he was unable personally to supervise the work and unlikely to live to see it completed. In accordance with his instructions, no inscription was affixed to the monument, nor reason given for its construction. It was hoped that the pyramid would stand, by its charming simplicity and beauty, an embellishment and benefit for the town in years to come. Was this then a mere whimsical folly on behalf of Mr Killigrew? Had he an interest in the Egyptian pyramids which prompted him to design his own memorial 480 inches high – virtually a twelfth of the height of the Great Pyramid of Cheops.

The monument is carefully designed to comprise three sections, the centre-most section 12ft wide at the base, 11ft wide at the top and 6ft high. The top section is 10ft wide at the base, tapering upwards as a slender pyramid between 25ft and 28ft high. The 14ft wide base section is now largely buried in the grass covered mound with only about 2ft protruding at the top. Since the overall height of the monument is given as 40ft, we may say that the base is either 6ft or 9ft tall, depending on the corresponding height of the top section.

Mr Killigrew seems to have taken a delight in furnishing the dimensions as they are "according to ye modell." Is there any secret geometry hidden in the construction to be revealed only to the inquiring mind? The tall standing stone is in a way like a signature, perhaps showing that one of the initiated few had passed this way. Before his marriage into the Killigrew family, Martin Killigrew had been known by the name of Lister, apparently of Liston in Staffordshire. He was born in 1666 which make him

a contemporary of a rather more mysterious figure –
The Count of St Germain.

Seen in 1710 by the composer Jean Phillipe
Rameau, St Germain appeared to be only about 45
years old, an apparent age he always maintained
although it is claimed that he lived for 150 years or
never died at all.

St. Germain, as a master alchemist, must be one of
the few who ever succeeded in making the 'Stone'.
He appeared mysteriously into European society,
where his conversation, wit and charm opened the
doors into the best of circles. He was much travelled
and endowed with occult wisdom, claiming to have
studied in the Pyramids. He was fabulously rich,
largely through his possession of the Philosopher's
Stone, which enabled him to transmute base metals
into gold. And was the source of the elixir of life
which gave him his longevity. He could also
improve and enlarge diamonds, which led to the
acquisition of a superb collection of gem stones.

Like many other alchemists, adepts and occultists,
St. Germain left behind a written work to inspire and
assist others who should search for the great Stone.
Like most of the other masters however, these
instructions are so cryptic and incomprehensible as
to be of little use except to those already in
possession of the sought-for knowledge.

Throughout the centuries, the search for the
philosopher's stone and the elixir of life has
occupied many people for their entire lifetimes. It
has also consumed family fortunes and cut some
lives shorter than they might otherwise have been
through lack of understanding of some fundamental
rules of chemistry. Even the celebrated Isaac

Newton suffered from metallic poisoning, particularly mercury and lead, as a recent analysis of a lock of his hair has shown. Newton used to sleep in his laboratory and as well as tasting some of his concoctions, inhaled fumes from his many experiments involving metals.

The alchemists, through their dabblings, and as a by-product, may have laid the foundations of modern chemistry, but the great goal is the Stone.

Production of the stone is known as the "Great Work" and although in the writings of the Masters we are presented with many clues, the trail is so concealed that without a key to the mysticism of the words or phrases used, the practical application of the instructions is not possible. The true object of the work is not the transmutation of any metal, but rather the transmutation of the Alchemist himself. That is to say, he hopes to achieve a higher spiritual plane.

This is achieved through the philosopher's stone which can be powdered and taken as a toxin to rejuvenate and prolong life. A by-product and also the test of whether the stone has been correctly manufactured is its ability to change base metals into gold. The steps involved in producing the stone are usually long and laborious.

One remarkable thing about the stone, is that when transforming metals, only a tiny speck is required. The metal, lead or mercury, is heated until melting point, then a speck of the stone powder, wrapped in paper or embedded in wax, is introduced to the molten metal. Transformation takes about 15 minutes.

The similarity between the use of a single grain of powder and the seeding of a crystal is striking.

With some crystal solutions, even though they are super-saturated and ripe for crystallisation, nothing will happen until a tiny 'seed' of the solid is introduced. Then the crystals may appear in a flash whereas without that initial seed to build upon, the solution might otherwise be kept indefinitely – crystal clear and clear of crystals! The seed which is introduced need not belong to the same substance as that in the solution but must resemble it close enough to belong to the same crystal class.

Although the methods by which the alchemists may have attempted their transmutations may today be seen as absurd, there is an underlying feeling of truth behind the idea that one metal can be changed into another. As long ago as the 13th century, Arnold Villanova in the "Path to the Way" was to write…

"Every body is made up of elements into which it may be resolved. Let us take an example that is impossible to refute and easy to understand. Ice, with the help of fire, can be resolved into water; therefore ice is water. Now, all the metals can be resolved into Mercury, therefore Mercury is the prime matter of all metals. At a later stage I shall demonstrate how the transmutation may be carried out thereby refuting the opinion of those who claim that the composition of metals cannot be changed. They would be right if it were impossible to reduce metals to their prime matter; but I shall show that reduction to prime matter is easy, and that transmutation is possible and practicable."

That which he calls "Mercury" is not the element of that name, but in the alchemical jargon, the basic substance into which all matter can be resolved. It is however notable that mercury should so early be identified with the prime matter, since in the chemical league table, Mercury is next to Gold with atomic numbers of 80 and 79 respectively. Mercury has 80 surrounding electrons and Gold only 79, whereas Lead has 82. Now if only Mercury could be persuaded to give up one electron.....

Gold has in fact been manufactured in a similar way in a modern nuclear laboratory, but the cost of the process is such as to make it un-economic.

Beyond Uranium, all known substances decay spontaneously, by emitting radiations. However a theory in the Soviet Union suggests that there may be stable, super-heavy elements beyond Uranium. One of these, Eka lead or Super-lead with an atomic number of 135 appears suitable for a transmutation into an isotope of gold.

The alchemists recognised three ways by which the Stone could be achieved, the Humid way – which took three years, the Dry way – a few weeks and the short way.

To Philalethes, author of "Fountain of Chymical Philosophy" – "Gold is the most perfect of all metals. It is the father of our stone, and yet it is not its prime matter; the prime matter of the stone is the germinative contained in gold."

Fulcanelli is one of the most recent alchemists, and disappeared leaving his pupil to publish his manuscript "Le Mystère des Cathedrals". In this difficult and typically cryptic work, "the stone is the foundation", and is illustrated as a pentagram, rather like the bishop's hat. "The stone is presented to us in the form of a clear, crystalline substance, red in the mass, yellow when pulverised. It is dense and highly fusible although solid at all temperatures, and its substance makes it penetrating, fiery, invariable and incombustible." To him a philosopher is "a man who knows how to make glass" – the dense alchemical glass of the cathedrals perhaps.

A visitor, possibly Fulcanelli, to the test lab of the Paris Gas Company supposedly said … "Will you allow me to give you a word of warning. The work that you and your colleagues are undertaking is appallingly dangerous. It imperils not only you personally but it is a threat to the whole of humanity. To release nuclei is easier than you think and artificial radio-activity can poison the atmosphere all over the Earth within a very few years. Atomic explosions can be created with a few grammes of metal, and can destroy whole cities. I am telling you this point blank. Alchemists have known it for a very long time. You think that alchemists do not know the structure of the nucleus, do not understand electricity, have no means of detection. So they have never achieved a transmutation, nor ever managed to release nuclear energy. I am not going to try to prove what I intend telling you now, but I would like you to repeat it to M. Hellbronner.

Geometrical arrangements of extremely pure substances suffice to loose atomic forces without the use of electricity or the vacuum technique. … You will not be unaware that in present day   official science, the part played by the observer becomes more and more important. Relativity, the principle of contingency, demonstrates how important is the role of the observer nowadays. The secret of Alchemy is that there exists a means of manipulating matter and energy so as to create what modern science calls a field of forces. The field of forces acts upon the observer and puts him in a privileged position over the unwise. From the privileged position he has access to realities that space and time, matter and energy, normally conceal from us. This is what we call the Great Work."

A report on the first use of the atom by the Military described it as "a geometrical arrangement of extremely pure substances". It is now acknowledged that the main obstacle to anyone building an explosive nuclear device is the acquisition of sufficiently pure 'substances' and knowing just how much to bring together … the critical mass…..

The first stage in the making of the Stone, from Cylianis' "Hermes Unveiled" is making the Philosophers Mercury.
"I chose a substance containing the two metallic elements. I first steeped it in astral spirit, very gradually, in order to rekindle its interior fires which seemed to be dead, by drying it slowly and pounding it in the mortar with a circular movement, all in the warmth of the Sun. I repeated this work a number of times, moistening it increasingly, drying and pounding, until the whole had become a fairly thick paste. Then I added a fresh quantity of astral spirit, enough to cover the solid matter, and left it to stand for five days, at the end of which I carefully poured

off the liquid into a bottle and stood it in a cool place; then again in the warmth of the Sun, I dried the substance that remained in the glass jar, which came about three fingers high. I steeped, pounded, dried and dissolved as before etc... stored in a stoppered jar which I put into the coldest place that I could find."

There are however seven regimens from "The open door into the secret palace of the king"….. "The first regimen of the work is that of Philosophic Mercury, the second Saturn or Lead, the third that of Jupiter or Tin, the fourth the Moon or Philosophic Silver, the fifth Venus or Copper, the sixth Mars or Iron and the seventh the Sun or Philosophic Gold.

At last on the 27th day of the regimen, it will begin to dryout, then liquify; will become fluid then congeal; and it will continue to liquify a hundred times a day until it becomes gritty, and the whole substance appears to split up into tiny granules.

Finally, at the command of God, the light in your matter will emit rays of such brilliance as you can hardly imagine. When you see this light, you may expect the end of your work to be near, for three days later you will see the completion for which you have striven, when the Matter will break up into small, very white granules as minute as motes in sunlight, and more beautiful than anything anyone has ever seen."

The reader is usually left to decipher and decide for himself the nature of the ingredients of the primes substance – which may vary according to whether the Way is long or short.

Aluminium, copper, lead, silver, gold and platinum all belong to the face-centred cubic, crystal structure. Mercury is rhombahedral and tin body-centred tetragonal at ordinary temperatures i.e. over 55°F. When white tin is kept at low temperatures it crumbles away to a grey powder and was described by Aristotle as 'melting'. The change to grey tin is a slow process even below freezing temperature but if the white tin is rubbed with a piece of grey tin, the grey tin supplies nuclei 'seeds' and the change-over is considerably more rapid.

An arcane body of knowledge was supposed to have existed from the Beginning, to be handed down to only the selected few and quite often in ways that the uninitiated would not understand.

The Alchemists were philosophers who resorted to physical experiments to achieve the Stone which would give them life, wealth and wisdom. Other philosophers of the Middle Ages purported to have access to the hidden or occult knowledge which revealed the mysteries of the Cosmos, from the workings of the Universe to the workings of a man's mind and body. The universe and the man belonged to the same heavenly order but differed in scale. Everything ordered on high was similarly ordered in the world of man, so that man himself and his planet the Earth, became the focal point of this universe.

This was continuing the tradition of Aristotle who had envisaged the universe as spherical with the stars fixed on an outermost sphere, the sun, moon and each planet attached to inner spheres, all rotating about a stationary Earth at the centre. Right up to the time of Copernicus and Kepler, ingenious, convincing mathematical solutions were offered to explain the movements of the heavenly bodies. Between the spheres lay the fifth element, the heavenly aether, and the Earth was composed of the four lesser elements; earth, water, fire and air.

Before Aristotle, the Pythagoreans had conceived a living universe, eternal and divine. Man was fallible and mortal, but his spirit was a fragment of the great Universal One, to which it could return after a succession of lower lives and having achieved spiritual perfection. The Kosmos was a perfectly ordered whole which included proportions, measure, beauty and harmony.

To the Pythagoreans, "all things are numbers", and everything could be rationalised into numerical arrangements, displayed geometrically and expanded to build up a network of points in space. In the musical scale, the intervals which are called the perfect consonants could be expressed numerically as the ratios between 1,2,3 and 4. The octave was produced by the ratio 2:1 (a note an octave higher than its predecessor has double its frequency, the fifth 3:2 and the fourth 4:3. The perfect Pythagorean number was ten and their sign, the five pointed star, incorporates the mathematical 'golden sections'.

The Atomic theory was first put forward by Leukippus and developed by his pupil Democritus from Thrace in northern Greece about 460BC. Democritus believed there could be no creation or destruction of any real thing, only a re-shuffling as it were, of things already in existence. The Void was acknowledged and all matter consisted of a multitude of tiny bodies – the atomoi. These particles were invisible, similar in composition but not in size or shape, existing and flitting through timeless space. By their conglomerations together they created matter which varied according to its constituent atoms.

The supreme God can be seen as Mind and Mind as Life. Anaxagoras of Athens around 456BC described Mind as the force and energy imparting motion to the constituents of matter, which has no inherent force of its own. The Supreme Mind then, is of a power to embrace all forms of matter and motion, life and existence.

A recent radio broadcast described Albert Einstein as "Last of the Scientists – First of the Magicians" and one of his former colleagues had this to say of him;

"He was a creative artist in his science..... He made breakthroughs, and in his work there were two dominant factors. I'm sure you wouldn't imagine what they are. He was of course the greatest scientist of the time, and the two factors that pushed him in his work, were, looking for simplicity and beauty and aesthetic attitude, and also a profoundly religious attitude as well. I was asking him about a certain theory and he said, 'In judging a theory, I ask myself, would I have made the world like that if I were God?' And you can see there a sort of criterion, that you won't find in the text books of what is the scientific method. It shows you in a way, a sort of religious compulsion to look at the Universe, which he regarded all his life with awe and amazement and admiration. He wanted to discover some of its secrets. He knew that it was much more mysterious than anything man can comprehend. When he made his discoveries, he did indeed seem to have caught something of the cosmic beauty, and, even when presenting some of these results to the Prussian Academy of Sciences, he said, 'Practically anyone who has really understood this theory, will be able to understand the attraction of its magic', - meaning, 'Isn't it wonderfully beautiful!' Actually, when it was finished, it was much more beautiful, you see."

"The human mind" Albert Einstein once said, "is not capable of grasping the Universe. We are like a little child," he continued, "entering a huge library. The walls are covered to the ceiling with books in many different tongues. The child knows that someone must have written these books. It does not know how or who. It does not understand the language in which they are written. But the child notes a definite plan in the arrangement of the books – a mysterious order which it does not comprehend but only dimly suspects."

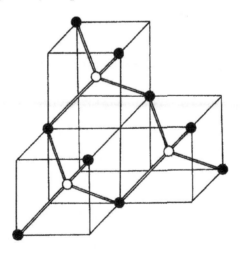

Chapter 3
Order in the Universe

THE THOUSANDS of megaliths surviving in Western Europe with their astronomical alignments show that man from a very early period engaged in the study of the stars. The Babylonians with their stepped pyramids also collated astronomical data as may well have the early Egyptians, but because these societies relied on an oral tradition of transmitting knowledge through their select priesthood no knowledge of their science has come down to us today.

Little of the writings of the early Greek thinkers still exist, but because their ideas were disseminated and developed in schools, their traditions have survived, albeit sometimes second-hand, and it is to them we give credit for the beginnings of the search to find an ordered structure in the movements of the celestial bodies. The ideas developed by the Greek philosophers were to hold sway right up to the end of the sixteenth century, when they were overturned by Copernicus' heliocentric (sun centred) theory which was finally established by Kepler. Even Kepler clung to the Pythagorean idea that everything was ordered according to harmony yet his search for a geometrical solution to the celestial problem did not hinder his researches but rather opened up new avenues of thought, his findings being based on the one thing the early Greeks had lacked – accurate observations.

At the commencement of Greek philosophy, the school established by Pythagoras had postulated that the centre of the universe was occupied by the Central Fire, around which the planets and stars revolved, but they failed to identify the central fire with the sun. To them the sun was merely one of the bodies revolving around this central point in space, along with the Earth, Moon, five planets, the sphere of the fixed stars, and of course, the Antichton – the counter Earth. The essence of the Pythagorean philosophy was that everything could be rationalised in terms of numbers harmonically arranged – to them ten was the perfect number. It was complete and consisted of the sum of the first four numbers. Accordingly, as they were one body short in their planetary system, they devised the Counter Earth or Double Earth to complete the planetary order. Each body on its travels was supposed to emit a tone so that collectively they produced a celestial harmony.

Pythagoras, the founder of the school, was born in Samos around 580BC and later travelled to the south of Italy where he established his school. A certain amount of religious mysticism attached itself to his school and he was sometimes revered as a god, reputedly having a golden thigh which he would occasionally show to admirers as a further proof of divine origins. He was said to have travelled extensively in the east and studied in Egypt and Babylon, from whence he acquired his not inconsiderable knowledge. He recognised the spherical form of the Earth although the credit for this is sometimes given to Parmenides, who may have taught it more openly. Parmenides arranged the Universe in the system of concentric spheres surrounding the Earth with the stars fixed to the outermost layer. This theme was more fully developed by Eudoxus of Knides, who produced the extremely refined system of homocentric spheres.

The poles of a sphere of a planet rotated independently within another larger sphere, which again was fixed in an independent fashion within an even larger sphere and so on. To account for all the celestial phenomena, it was necessary to introduce three spheres for the sun and moon and four spheres for each of the five planets, whilst the stars remained fixed to the outermost sphere, a grand total of twenty-seven spheres. This was intended more as a mathematical concept for predicting the movements of the heavenly bodies than as a fixed idea of what actually existed in space. It was later carried to extremes by Aristotle who expanded the number of spheres to fifty-five.

Plato, one of the most respected of the ancient philosophers was more interested in politics than astronomy. He supported the idea of a powerful city-state with a rigidly organised class structure into which everyone should fit. To introduce his theories he produced several dialogues between eminent statesmen, with all the incidental details closely and cleverly worked out. In his tribute to Socrates, the earth is described as standing freely in the midst of heaven, round like a twelve-striped leather ball. His machinery for moving the heavens around the earth consisted of a great spindle driven by Necessity. A core of light extended through the universe and the central earth. Each planet had a circle surrounding the earth and on each of these circles a Siren was seated, emitting a note so that the eight sirens completed the Harmony. The three daughters of necessity, the Fates of Past, Present and Future sang to the tune of the harmony and took turns to drive the spindle, laying hold of the circles, one turning the outer circle, another, the inner circles and the third driving the outer and inner circles in turn. In the Timaeus, he describes how the Great Artificer created the spherical world and placed it on the axis stretching through the universe. The sun was provided on the second orbit to provide light for all who desired to perceive the Order.

Aristotle, 384-322BC attempted to review and summarise all the preceding philosophical ideas in the light of his own interpretations derived largely from the meanings of words and immediately observable natural phenomena. The outermost of his fifty-five spheres is considered to be the most perfect sphere since as well as containing all the others, it drives the celestial machinery. He cannot accept that anything but the earth lies at the centre of all this and sets the stage for the next 1800 years by proclaiming the earth stationary at the centre of the universe.

The geocentric system of Aristotle was to be polished up finally by Ptolemy of Alexandria before being handed down to the middle ages, but before this, two other Greeks had come very close to the truth.

A contemporary of Aristotle, Herakleides of Pontus taught that the earth turned on its axis in twenty-four hours and adopted what was known as the 'Egyptian' system of letting Mercury and Venus move around the sun. Aristarchus of Samos 281BC also believed that Mercury and Venus had heliocentric orbits and may have considered this motion for all the planets since he proposed the sun as the centre of the universe with the earth moving in an oblique circle and turning on its own axis. This system won little support in the face of the established system of Aristotle, the numerous spheres seeming necessary to account for all the celestial phenomena and the system of Aristarchus failed because of its simplicity.

Ptolemy consolidated the work of the earlier Greeks, particularly Hipparchus of Rhodes, who 300 years earlier worked on the theory of epicycles and discovered the precession of the equinoxes from Alexandrine and Babylonian observations. Ptolemy completed the planetary theory using the earlier observations which he adjusted with an incorrect figure for precession and accepted the planetary order attributed to the ancients from Babylon – Moon, Mercury, Venus, Sun, Mars, Jupiter and Saturn.

The Dark Ages were ushered in by the burning of the library at Alexandria by the Christian mob in 389AD, shortly after the barbarians had over-run Europe. The guardians of the church stuck literally to the word of the Scriptures, the description of Genesis being the appointed view of the Beginning. The system of Aristotle was initially discredited then later adopted as the only tolerated system. Speculations as to the size of the earth and the planetary systems were discouraged and as late as 1600AD, Giordano Bruno was burned at the stake for the heresy of suggesting that the sun rotated and that the fixed stars were also suns.

Copernicus spent twelve years revising his planetary theory, not daring to publish it until he was near the end of his life. The publication was released and a copy reached him on the day he died. Nicholas Copernicus was born in 1473, the son of a wealthy merchant of Thorn, in Poland. His father died early and it was under the guidance of his maternal uncle, the influential Bishop of Ermland that Nicholas and his elder brother, Andrzej, entered the monastery of Cracow in 1491. At Cracow, he received his first introduction to astronomy, not the subject for which he had been enrolled, but one for which the university was renowned. His uncle intended to confer a canonry on Nicholas and after Cracow, he suggested that Nicholas follow in his own footsteps by continuing his studies at the university of Bologna. Accordingly Nicholas went to Bologna in Italy in January 1497 where he was to spend three and a half years as a student of canon law. Here Copernicus took a great interest in the writings of the ancient Greeks and developed his interest in astronomy, Bologna being closely linked to Cracow in the fields of astronomy and mathematics. In 1501 Copernicus returned home to be confirmed in the canonry of Frauenberg and immediately obtained his leave of absence to return to Italy and further his studies. This time he went to Padua, where in addition to canon law he studied medicine for which he later became quite famous. He took his degree as a doctor of canon law at the university of Ferrara in 1503 and three years later returned to Ermland where he was to spend the rest of his life.

Copernicus had been well versed in the classics and from the varying and conflicting accounts of the celestial systems left by the writers of old, had sensed that none of them had grasped the true theory. By a penetrating study of all the writings available he found that some of the Greek writers had contemplated letting the planets revolve around a Central Fire. Copernicus realised that the sun was a central fire and thus the heliocentric theory was born – or reborn. The new theory was first broadcast in the form of a short essay, with a very limited circulation since all the copies were hand written. Whereas it was essentially correct in asserting that the earth moved around the sun like any other planet, Copernicus did not feel that it adequately represented the apparent movements of the planets and it was about thirty years later that the Copernicus system was completed. This system was incorrect in as much as he assumed all the planets to have perfectly circular orbits, and these required numerous epicycles just as Ptolemy's had done. Copernicus was actively engaged with his duties as a canon and also in considerable demand for his knowledge of medicine. He made some observations but lacked the necessary refined instruments and it was only by a long process of accurate observations that the new theory could be proved or refuted.

The foundations of the new astronomy were made by Tycho Brahe from his observatory on the Danish island of Hven. Tycho, a Dane of noble birth, had entered the Leipzig university to study law but had developed more than a passing interest in astronomy. He began to be known as an astronomer and after giving lectures in Copenhagen at the royal request he was shortly after granted the island of Hven together with the funds to build an observatory. Tycho equipped it with huge measuring instruments to his own designs, plotted the positions of hundreds of stars and tracked the movements of the planets and occasional comet.

On the death of King Frederick II, Tycho found himself alienated from the rest of the Danish nobility and for fear of his observations being confiscated for the state, took flight to Germany. He found a new patron in the person of the Holy Roman Emperor, Rudolph II who allowed him the use of the castle of Benatky and promised to build him an observatory. Tycho never fully accepted the Copernican system and was to an extent influenced by the church doctrine of the time. Instead he cleverly compromised with a system of his own, which was mathematically identical to that of Copernicus, but proclaimed that all the planets revolved around the sun which again revolved around the earth. When Tycho bequeathed his tables of observations to Kepler, he insisted that they be published in accordance with his own theory and not that of Copernicus. Kepler, although for a time Tycho's assistant and collaborator, was an adherent of the Copernican heliocentric system and the tables were eventually published with an explanation of the systems of Ptolemy, Copernicus and Tycho Brahe. Tycho had shattered the idea of the crystalline spheres by demonstrating that comets were interplanetary bodies but Kepler was the man who finally established the true motions of the earth and other planets.

If Pythagoras was the man who started the search for order in the universe, then Kepler was the man who found it. John Kepler was named after the apostle of St. John, being born on St. John's day, 1571. He came from a poor family and was always to be handicapped by domestic problems. His father absconded to the Low Countries in the service of the military and his mother was later to be tried as a witch. He started his career as a theological student and after attending the Latin school at Laeonburg he entered the university of Tubingen, which was then housed in an old Augustinian monastery. His two years leading to a masters degree on a faculty of arts course were followed by three more on the subject of theology. Kepler remained always aloof from the other scholars, particularly as he depended solely on grants with no spare money for the usual student activities. He found an interest devising horoscopes and calendars and because of his ability as a mathematician coupled with his rebellious attitude towards the established church doctrines he was put forward in 1594 to a post as teacher of mathematics at the protestant seminary in Graz.

Whilst lecturing to his pupils, Kepler drew an illustration to show the conjunctions of Saturn and Jupiter that take place every 20 years and this brought to mind the five regular solids which he thought might more properly take the place of the celestial spheres.

Kepler believed in the Universal Harmony and that everything had been ordered by the Divine Creator. He was to devote the remainder of his life to a search for an ordered relationship between the

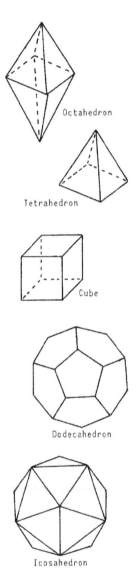

Octahedron

Tetrahedron

Cube

Dodecahedron

Icosahedron

distances and movements of the planets and the pursuance of his geometric theories led to his great discoveries. The mathematical notion of a sphere or spheres surrounding each planet was given a new dimension by Kepler, who, realising that there were (then known) six planets with five spaces between them, sought to ascribe one of the five regular polyhedra to each of these spaces. These five regular solids had been discovered by the Pythagoreans who had proved that only five polyhedra exist which display a complete regularity of faces and edges. They are the cube, with six square faces, eight corners 12 edges and 24 plane angles; the tetrahedron with four equilateral triangles, the octahedron with eight triangles, the dodecahedron with 12 regular pentagons and the icosahedron with 20 triangles. These were sometimes called the "platonic" bodies after Plato, who had mentioned them in connection with the Universe. If we were to fit, say, an octagon within a circle, then by joining the points of the octagon we would find a smaller circle enclosed which would have a fixed ratio relative to the outer circle.

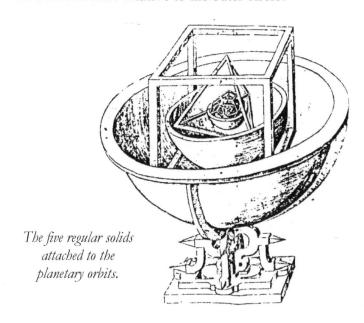

The five regular solids attached to the planetary orbits.

Similarly, the sphere surrounding a regular solid has a fixed ratio in relation to the sphere that would be contained inside the solid, in its simplest form a sphere containing a cube to the sphere contained within the cube.

Thus the orbit of Saturn enclosed a cube containing the orbit of Jupiter. From Jupiter, a tetrahedron to Mars, a dodecahedron to earth, an icosahedron to Venus and an octahedron to Mercury.

Kepler announced his new theory in a book in support of Copernicus' heliocentric system, recognising that all the planets should behave in a similar manner under the control of a force emanating from the sun, entitled "The Cosmographic Mystery". He sent copies to friends, also to Galileo, who acknowledged it but was in no position to encourage it, and to Tycho Brahe, who thus became aware of Kepler's potential as a mathematician.

Two years later, Kepler was expelled from Graz in a religious purge by the Archduke Ferdinand and in pursuit of data to prove his regular solids theory he accepted Tycho's invitation to join him at his recently established observatory in Prague. Tycho allocated him the task of constructing the orbit of Mars, which led to Kepler's discovery that a planet's velocity depends on its distance from the sun and that its orbit is actually an ellipse and not as previously thought, a circle. The degree of oscillation is quite small, so that the orbit has virtually the appearance of a circle, the Earth for example being at closest 91½ million miles and at furthest 94½ million miles from the sun.

The death of Tycho in 1601 resulted in Kepler being appointed his successor as imperial mathematician. Kepler should now have had all the data he required but access to Tycho's notes was for a time blocked by his heirs. His first two laws, that a planet moves in an elliptical orbit with the sun occupying one of the foci and that the radius vector of a planet describes equal area in equal time were published in the "New Astronomy" of 1609.

In addition to domestic troubles, Kepler experienced financial difficulties, the post at Prague being by nature honorary rather than lucrative. Following the demise of the Emperor Rudolph II in 1611, Kepler took up a post as district mathematician at Linz in Austria. He remained there for fourteen years before being again harassed by Ferdinand, who had become Emperor.

As a tribute to a patron, the Duke of Wurtemburg, Kepler wrote an essay on the structure of snow crystals. Perceiving them to be the work of the divine hand, he pointed out their hexagonal structure, which reminded him of the geometrical structure of the honeycomb. The cells of the honeycomb were arranged in a fashion similar to a number of spheres packed closely together and anticipates the crystalline structure of most solids.

From the many observations of Kepler and Tycho Brahe, the regular solids theory proved to be at best a somewhat loose fit, even allowing a certain thickness to each sphere to accommodate the elliptical orbit. Kepler then took up the 'music of the spheres' as the underlying mathematical concept of the heavenly order. This proved a greater success and allowed the positions of the planets to be plotted according to musical notation. Under this system, the wide gap between Mars and Jupiter was particularly noticeable, a gap which Kepler had earlier tried to fill by introducing a hypothetical planet to support his previous theories. Kepler differed from the Pythagoreans in that he believed the tone was generated not by the distance ratio of a planet but by its angular velocity and associated elliptical orbit. His investigation of the numerical ratio of the orbits and distances led him to his last great discovery, that the squares of the periods of the planets are proportional to the cubes of their mean distances from the sun.

Kepler wrote to Galileo seeking an interchange of ideas and was keenly interested in the telescopes manufactured and made popular by Galileo. Kepler, with his mathematical flair, designed a superior type of lens arrangement but no collaboration was forthcoming.; Galileo, being closer to the seat of Papal authority, had more to fear in the way of retributions. His observations using the telescope with its 30X magnification proved that the stars were much more distant than the planets since they always remained minute points of light, whereas the planets were enlarged and their moons could be identified. In reply to Kepler's "Cosmographic Mystery", Galileo wrote that he had always believed in the Copernican system but did not dare admit it publicly. When as a result of his own observations he was finally convinced of the truth of this system, he broadcast it publicly and was consequently banned by the church. In 1616 he was banned from spreading the Copernican ideas and in 1633 had to face the Inquisition on a charge of heresy, for which he had to recant his theories and was to be confined thereafter to his villa with no further public communication.

Kepler's last refuge was at Sagen, where he went at the invitation of the Duke, who had a strong interest in astrology. The Rudolphine Tables were published in 1627 with a dedication to the former patron who had brought he and Tycho Brahe together and Kepler died in the course of a hazardous journey undertaken in the winter of 1630.

Chapter 4

The Great Pyramid

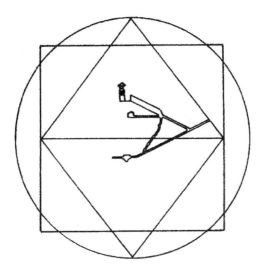

OF ALL the wonders of the ancient world the Great Pyramid is not only the most impressive, it has proved to be the most enduring. Built around 4,600 years ago for the pharaoh Khufu (in Greek, Cheops), it has also proved to be the most controversial. The argument centres on whether the pyramid was built solely as a funeral tomb for a king, or whether it was built as the architectural masterpiece of a lost science.

On the one side it is quoted as the most monumental folly in the history of mankind, impressive mainly because of the tremendous amount of effort expended to heap up such a useless pile of stones, enough stones to build a wall 'x' times around France or the circumference of the Earth. It is even said to have failed in its task of preserving the body of the king as no body has been found in the pyramid.

Amongst the claims for the other side are that the pyramid incorporates the value of pi 3.141592653 and phi 1.618 (the golden section); it is supposedly built in pyramid inches related to the diameter of the earth; its sides are aligned to true north; it is a model of the northern hemisphere; the length of the perimeter gives the days in a year; the height gives the distance from the sun; it contains a universal system of weights and measures and the dimensions of the inner galleries foretell the future of mankind.

Factually, we can say at least one thing about the Great Pyramid, it is a ruin. Externally that is, for the interior appears never to have been properly finished. The pyramid was once encased in gleaming white limestone, but the centuries have taken their toll and the beautiful casing stones were removed long ago to furnish material for other building projects.

Any survey of the building has first of all to try and determine the exact location of the corners of the structure, and the resultant figures have to be interpreted in the light of the measure being used i.e. metres, feet, cubits or whatever, and bearing in mind that even today, different geodetic figures are given by different authorities. The differences are only slight, but enough to uphold or refute the case for or against the scientific origins of the pyramid. It will become apparent later that it is insufficient to talk in terms of inches or millimetres, but that the argument hinges around fractions of a millimetre.

The great period of pyramid building lasted only about a hundred years. It began with the stepped pyramid at Saqqara and terminated in the pyramid of Menkaure, the third and smallest of the pyramids on the Giza plateau. This was during the third and fourth dynasties of what is known as the old Kingdom. The old kingdom was followed by an intermediate period when most of the pyramids and tomb complexes were broken into and pilfered by people who were apparently in possession of plans of the structures, for they usually tunnelled directly into the inner chambers.

The first recorded entry into the Great Pyramid was in 820AD, at the orders of the Caliph Abdullah Al Mamun. This Arabian prince came not in search of the gold and silver treasures one might expect, but in order to find the terrestrial maps and globes, made in the remotest antiquity, which were reported to be secreted in the pyramid.

Al Mamun tunnelled over 100ft into the pyramid before coming across the descending passage which leads to a pit, 600ft below the apex of the pyramid. The pit was empty. Judging by scorch marks on the roof, it had already been visited in the past. On their way down the passage, the workmen had accidentally dislodged a stone concealing what appeared to be a passage leading up into the pyramid. Al Mamun now turned his attention to the ascending passage and began to attack the large granite block which effectively plugged the entrance. The only way past this obstacle was to tunnel around it and a succession of others which barred the way to the inner chambers.

At the top of the ascending passage, a horizontal passage led to a chamber, 18ft 10ins by 17ft 2ins and 20ft 5ins high, lying directly beneath the apex of the pyramid. This chamber was empty and on account of the shape of the roof was called the "Queens" chamber, by the Arabs. re-tracing their steps along the horizontal passage, the men found themselves back at the ascending passage, which opens into the Grand Gallery, 157ft long and 28ft high., sloping up into the pyramid and leading to what has proved so far to be the only other chamber, the "King's Chamber".

This room, 34ft by 17ft and 19ft high contained only one item, a lidless granite coffer, 6ft 6ins long on the inside. The granite of the coffer was even harder than that of the walls of the chamber and was reported to have been quarried not in Egypt, but in the legendary Atlantis.

The disappointed Arabs were paid of by Al Mamun and the pyramid slumbered on for a further four centuries before serving as a quarry for the city of Cairo.

Fortunately the task of destroying a pyramid is almost as hard as building one. Once the protective casing stones are removed, the pyramid is vulnerable to the ravages of the weather, but the sheer bulk of the stones defies the (by comparison) puny efforts of the later generations to reduce the monument.

The first scientific investigation into the dimensions of the pyramid took place in 1638, when John Greaves set out from London, specially equipped with a 10ft measuring rod finely divided into 10,000 parts. This was the age of the renaissance. Greaves had already spent some time in Italy measuring the ancient monuments of the Romans and found the Roman foot to be 24/25ths of the Greeks foot. Greaves hoped to find a datum which would enable him to compute the correct circumference of the planet, although at this period the world was widely held to be flat. Indeed, it was even considered a heresy to suggest the world was round; such was the decline experienced through the dark ages.

From an analysis of the measurements taken by Greaves in the King's chamber, Newton concluded that a 'profane' cubit of 20.63 inches had been used giving a chamber of 20 x 10 cubits. He also suspected the presence of a 'sacred' cubit of 25 inches which he calculated on the basis of the description of the Temple at Jerusalem. Newton was also interested to obtain the precise dimensions of the planet in order to confirm his theory of

gravitation. He needed to know the exact value of
the geographic degree and according to the ancient
historians, this value was built into the apothem of
the pyramid, which was said to equal a stadium or
1/10th of a degree.

During Napoleon's conquest of Egypt, his
Savants had ample time to survey and analyse the
pyramid. They found it to lie on an axis which
neatly bisected the Nile delta and angles extended
from the corners of the pyramid enclosed this fan-
shaped area. Jomard, the foremost of the savants,
measured down each step to obtain a height of 481ft.
He had already cleared away the debris from one
side of the base and obtained a figure of 757.5ft, so
now he could calculate the length of the sloping side
and the angle of the slope. He found the angle to be
almost the angle of pi and the length of the apothem
to be virtually the classical stadium of antiquity.

The geographic or "Greek" stadium of 600ft was
a 10th of a minute of latitude and comprised 400
geographic cubits of 1.5ft. The classics also reported
that the perimeter of the base of the pyramid was
intended to be half a degree of longitude. The
ancient Greek writers credited Egypt as the home of
mathematics and geometry, both Plato and
Pythagoras having studied there.

Jomard's colleagues re-measured the base and
apothem of the pyramid, obtained a different set of
figures and declared his findings invalid.

At the turn of the century, Sir John Herschel
recommended that the only truly scientific unit of
measure would be to take the polar diameter of the

planet, which the Ordnance Survey had fixed at 500,000,000 inches and break this down into units of sacred cubits of 25". This gave 10,000,000 sacred cubits as the polar radius of the planet and because of the relationship of this unit to the English inch, he concluded that the English inch was a sacred or scientific inch which had lost one part in a thousand through the ages.

Piazzi Smyth, astronomer royal for Scotland, believed passionately that the inch was a god-given measure handed down through the centuries from the time of Israel. Both Smyth and John Taylor, who had analysed the figures for the pyramid and found the pi relationship, considered that the pyramid could only have been built by Divine revelation and that the architect must have been directed by the hand of God. Smyth bitterly opposed the introduction of the French metre into Britain and succeeded in blocking its adoption through the houses of parliament.

At the end of 1864 Smyth set out for Egypt to measure the pyramid for himself. Like Greaves before him, he was also equipped with special instruments to take accurate measurements. Smyth also found the pyramid to be precisely orientated to true north and considered it to have been founded at a time when the pole star could be sighted through the ascending passage and the Pleides were directly overhead at midnight, giving a possible date of 3440BC. By direct measurement Smyth found the pi angle of 51.85 degrees in the casing stones and the pi ratio, 3.14159 in the perimeter of the base. He also found the perimeter of the base to equal the number of days in a year in inches, found the pyramid to rise from its base in a ratio of 1:9 and multiplied its height to give a figure equal in statute miles to the earth's distance from the sun.

Because of Smyth's mixing of religious and scientific theories, fuelled by additional theories that the gallery of the great pyramid foretold the destiny of mankind, his data was largely discredited and it was left to a professional surveyor to establish again the precise dimensions of the pyramid.

In 1880, Flinders Petrie set out for Egypt to measure the pyramid. He had his own specially made surveying equipment, designed by his father to be an improvement on the already sophisticated equipment used by Smyth. The great difficulty was still to locate the exact corners of the pyramid. Petrie's approach was to triangulate the entire plateau complex, setting up stations out and around the plateau and sighting back through his 10 inch theodolite.

Petrie found the base line of the pyramid to be 9069 inches and not the 9140 inches claimed by Smyth. This meant that the pyramid fell short of the required 36524.22″ to relate to the days in a year, but it should be mentioned that Smyth measured to the edge of a short platform surrounding the pyramid and it was debatable as to whether the edge of the platform or the edge of the first sloping stone marked the extremities of the monument.

Petrie also rejected the 25″ cubit of Smyth and established the existence of a royal cubit of 20.63″ giving a base of 440 cubits and a height of 280 cubits. By a careful study of the dimensions of the King's chamber, Petrie found that it not only incorporated the pi value of the exterior, but also the sacred Pythagorean 3-4-5 triangles. He also discovered that the square of the diagonals of the chambers were arranged in multiples of 10 square cubits.

Petrie concluded that not only did the pyramid embody a system of advanced mathematics, but that the actual task of cutting and placing the stones had been executed with what might be described as 'optical' precision.

In their search for the English inch in the great pyramid, Smyth and Taylor may have made one elementary mistake – they chose the wrong pyramid! They would have done better to have examined the first pyramid built and trace the development of the pyramid from the stepped mastaba at Saquarra to the last pyramid on the Giza plateau. The question would then become, who built it, who was the architect, what measures did he use and where did he come from?

Pyramid building in Egypt began under the third dynasty king, Zoser. The architect was Imhotep, who is generally recognised as a brilliant mathematician, builder, astronomer and was a priest of Heliopolis. It seems likely that Imhotep, who was later raised to Divine status and considered to be the son of Ptah, may well have conceived and designed the Great Pyramid although he may not have been around to see it built. His tomb has never been found.

If the measure used for the base of the first pyramid had a scientific origin, then it must have been obtained well in advance of the 'pyramid age', for although a pyramid can be used as an observatory, the data is available only after the structure has been built.

The temple complex at Heliopolis was probably the most ancient in Egypt. It was reputedly built on the first site available after the Chaos and was dedicated – as the name implies, to Helios – the sun. It was the home of mathematics, astronomy and the calendar and in its centre stood a massive stone obelisk which could be used for such calculations.

The first structure which Imhotep built was the largest monument in stone ever attempted in Egypt up to that time. It has been described as 63 metres square and 8 metres high with a slightly curved roof. ("The Mystery of the Pyramids" by Evans gives the length as 65 metres). In inches the base would have been pretty close to 2,500″ or 100 sacred cubits of 25″ covering one sacred acre. The perimeter of the base would accordingly be 100,000″ and the height, the pi figure of 3.141 x 100....in inches. This was the foundation of what was to become the stepped pyramid of Sokar, god of orientation. The first structure was probably intended to be the finished monument since it was dressed in polished limestone. However, the project was evidently successful, since it mushroomed by a further five building stages to become the stepped pyramid almost 197ft high.

It would seem that in the early days of pyramid building, the technique was experimentally feeling its way. A second step pyramid was commenced near Saqqara and a third about 20 miles further north. Neither of these was completed. These pyramid projects demanded a vast labour force and administration. This was beneficial to the economy of Egypt at that time since it helped transform independent groups of tribesmen by giving them a sense of national identity. Because of the size of the buildings, it seems likely that more than one pyramid was under construction at any given time.

It was usually left to a new pharaoh to finish the work of his predecessor and it appears that this was sometimes done less enthusiastically than when working on his own pyramid. It also appears that if we count the number of pharaohs available to be entombed, there are more pyramids available than pharaohs, Snofru for example had three major pyramids. The internal chamber was often too small to comfortably contain a human body and there is no record of a pharaoh of that period having been found inside a pyramid.

The fourth pyramid, which was the first to be changed from the stepped core to a true pyramid with sloping sides was at Meidum, out in the desert 40 miles south of Saqqara and the capital, Memphis. It may have been designed initially by Imhotep and was successfully built as a seven stepped structure of a similar height to the one at Saqqara, incorporating a passage aligned to the polar star. It was finished in polished limestone and rose at an angle of about 75°. This pyramid was later enlarged to become an eight-stepped pyramid and then finally, it was enlarged yet again to become a pyramid with an angle of slope of 52°. This last stage was never completed, for the new mantle collapsed and fell away from the smooth sides of the inner core.

Undeterred by this reversal, the pyramid builders pressed on with their next pyramid, which was probably already under construction, at Dashur. Possibly as a safety precaution, they reduced the angle of this pyramid from 54° to the angle of 43.5°, giving it the appearance of the 'bent' pyramid. This effectively reduced the height from a projected 443ft to around 330ft.

The pyramid which incorporated the pi angle of 51.85° is such that its height stands in relation to its perimeter as the radius to the circumference of a circle, i.e. 2Пr. The intention at Dashur may have been for the height to be 120 yards of 33″ (a unit found in Sumeria and the Indus Valley, where it was known as a gaz), but it is equally possible that, in the absence of a precise figure, the height should be multiplied by 2П to indicate a circle of 25,000″ or 1,000 sacred cubits. The actual perimeter of the base is 30,000″ which is 1200 sacred cubits of 25″ or 1,000 cubits or steps of 30″.

A second pyramid was built at Dashur, this time at the reduced angle of 43.5° and covering an area slightly larger than the bent pyramid. It contained three chambers and entrance was by a passage aligned to the polar star.

After the pyramids at Dashur came the architectural masterpiece, the Great Pyramid of

Khufu (Cheops), the largest and the finest, with the correct pi angle of 51°51'14.3".

Khufu's death led to a certain amount of disruption in the royal household. He was succeeded not by a true royal prince, but by Djedfre, one of his sons by a secondary queen. Djedfre chose a remote inaccessible rock five miles north of Giza for his pyramid The pyramid was quite small, with a side of only 318.3ft. Multiply this side by the pi figure and it cunningly becomes 12,000 inches – 1,000ft exactly.

Djedfre was followed after eight years by another of Khufu's sons, Khafre, called in Greek, Chepren. His pyramid is comparable in size to Cheops and has a base diagonal of 12,000 inches.

The last and smallest of the pyramids on the Giza plateau is that of Menkaure, Khafre's son. Its base diagonal is 6,000 inches and its height when multiplied by pi is 420 royal cubits, the same as the base side of the red pyramid at Dashur..

The Great Pyramid has been likened to a scale model of the northern hemisphere.

One should expect the perimeter of the base to equate to equatorial longitude, the height to the polar radius and the apothem, or slant height, to the mean figure for latitude. But if the pyramid were 'simply' an exact scale model with base and height as described, then it could not incorporate the true figure for pi, since the Earth is not a true sphere but something of an oval or pear shape.

If the angle of slope were to incorporate the true pi figure, then the pyramid would express the pi values of the sphere and circle, but it would lose its

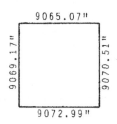

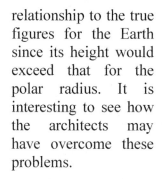

relationship to the true figures for the Earth since its height would exceed that for the polar radius. It is interesting to see how the architects may have overcome these problems.

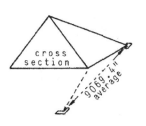

In 1925, Ludwig Borchard, director of the German Institute of Archaeology in Cairo, commissioned a professional engineer to make a survey of the Great Pyramid and finally resolve the question of its dimensions.

The survey was carried out by J.H.Cole. After the debris had been cleared away, he carefully established the four corner positions and obtained the following measurements (25.4mm to the inch)

North side 9065.08″
South side 9072.99″
East side 9070.51″
West side 9069.18″

Additionally, he found a mark on the northern pavement, breaking this side into two segments, 4531.1″ to the west and 4533.9″ to the east, suggesting that the apex of the pyramid was deliberately displaced about 1½″ off centre.

The base of the pyramid is therefore not a true square and the angles of its corners are accordingly, marginally more or less than 90°. The average figure for a side of the pyramid is 9069.44″

Before attempting to do any calculations with the dimensions of the pyramid, there are other considerations to be borne in mind. Each corner of the pyramid rests in a socket and it can be argued as to whether these sockets should be included in the dimensions for the base of the pyramid. The south-west socket is just over 20″ wide and can be extended to form a platform right around the pyramid. The north-west and north-east sockets are just over 30″ and the south-east socket about 35.5″. By measuring to the extremes of the sockets, Piazzi Smyth had obtained the figure in inches related to the days in a year.

Another complication is that each face of the pyramid is slightly hollowed towards the centre, by about perhaps 37″. We could then consider whether the true length of a side is the distance sighted directly from corner to corner, or the slightly increased distance measured along the actual stonework.

The ancients reported that the perimeter of the base was half a minute of degree and the apothem, a stadium or tenth of a minute of degree. As the total length of the apothem would actually exceed a stadium, the topmost section was distinguished in the form of a mini-pyramid or pyramidon. This pyramidon could then be included or excluded from the calculations as required.

So what kind of minute of degree has been built into the perimeter of the base?

At the equator, a minute of longitude is 6087.2ft and a minute of latitude is 6046.3ft.

Because of the shape of the Earth, the value of a minute of altitude increases all the way up to the North Pole, where it is 6107.8ft.

If a unit of measurement, such as the foot, is derived from a minute of latitude, then it will vary according to where this value is determined. Thus the Greek foot is larger than the Egyptian foot and so on.

The mean figure for a minute of latitude is 6076.8884ft – taken as 6080ft by the British Admiralty for the nautical mile then in recent times reduced to 6076ft.

The pyramid, with a mean side of 9069.4″ gives a minute of 6046.27ft (1842.9m) which compares to the
6046.35ft (1842.925m) of the International Spheroid and the
6045.89ft (1842.787m) of the Clarke Spheroid for a minute of latitude at the equator.

So from Cole's survey, the mean perimeter of the base of the pyramid is half a minute of latitude at the equator – not the half a minute of longitude as we had expected.

As there are 360 x 60 x 2 half-minutes in a circle, then the scale of the pyramid is 1:43200.

The side of the base is reported to have been 440 cubits and the height of the pyramid 280 cubits. So how long is a cubit? Like the proverbial piece of string, it is any length convenient for the purpose in hand and has theoretical values from the geographic cubit of 18″ to the full great cubit of 30″.

One of the best sources of information on the Great Pyramid is the book "Secrets of the Great Pyramid" by Peter Tomkins with a comprehensive section on ancient measures by Livio Steccini.

Steccini found three values of Egyptian Royal Cubit in the pyramid complex.

Royal cubit 1   20.635″ (524.1483mm) of the king's chamber
Royal cubit 2   20.669″ (525mm) from Kephren's pyramid
Royal cubit 3   20.72″ (526.3231mm) of the coffer related to volume.

The normal Egyptian cubit was the cubit of 450mm which consisted of 6 palms. This cubit was 1½ Egyptian feet of 300mm. The addition of a seventh palm made the Royal cubit of 525mm.

If we take the base side of 9073″ and divide by 440, we have a royal cubit of 20.62″. When considered as the side of a square, this cubit gives rise to a diagonal of 2 remen which is said to be the length swung by a pendulum, 100,000 times in

24hrs at the latitude of the ancient capital of Memphis.

Conversely, a square of side 1 remen, will have a diagonal of 2 royal cubits. The Egyptian remen of 14.58″ was used for land surveying and is a 5,000th part of the mean figure for a minute of latitude.

The 2:1 rectangle is particularly interesting because from it the value of phi can be obtained. Consider the rectangle as two squares side by side. The first square is further divided vertically into two rectangles. The diagonal of the right-hand rectangle is then swung down to the base of the right-hand square, which it divides in the ratio of .618 thus splitting the complete rectangle in the ratio of 1.618.

This division of the rectangle gives rise to a logarithmic spiral and the ratio known as the Golden Section, found in the five-pointed star and preserved in many classical buildings and works of art. It is also expressed in the pyramid where the surface area of a face of the pyramid is equal to the square on the height and in the 2:1 ratio of the king's chamber.

The angle of slope for pi is 51°51′14.3″ and for phi is 51°49′ 38″.

The marginal difference in angles may be enough to account for the slight displacement of the apex off true centre, so that each side preserves a different set of values.

Since several feet are missing from the top of the pyramid, we can only estimate its height and calculate what it ought to have been. Jomard found it to be 481ft. From the dimensions of the base, we can say that it was between 480 and 484ft.

Hutchinsons 20th century encyclopaedia gives the polar diameter of the Earth as 7,900 statute miles. To be a 43200th part of the polar radius, the height of the pyramid would need to be

$$\frac{3959 \text{ statute miles x } 5280\text{ft}}{43200} = 482.77\text{ft}$$

If we calculate the height from pi and the length of the base, then the average side of 9069.4″ gives a height of 481.15ft.

From the base and the height we could now consider the length of the apothem. This is the slant height of the pyramid – the distance from the apex to half-way along the base side. We have a choice of base sides for our calculation, and should we allow for the 'hollowing' effect on each side to obtain the true apothem? If we had to subtract the amount of hollowing per side, then the 'inner base' would be nearer 9,000″ - a very attractive figure for the architect since it implies the ideal perimeter of 36,000″.

The mean perimeter of the base has been found to have a value related to the degree of latitude at the equator, so what degree of latitude would the architect choose for the apothem? Which standard did he wish to preserve?

Since the top is missing we are presented with a choice of two equations.

If the height were the true polar figure of 482.77ft, then with a base side of 9073″ the apothem would theoretically be 613.18ft. The pyramidon is reported as 4 cubits, so subtract 4 Royal Cubits of 525mm and the remaining apothem is a stadium of 606.3 English feet (184.8m) comprising 600 geographic feet of 308mm. This foot is derived from the latitude of Babylon and seems to have been used as a standard by navigators throughout the Mediterranean.

The pyramid was intended to symbolise the value of pi. The mean side of 9069.4″ gives by pi a height of 481.15ft and an apothem of 611.8ft (184.67m) giving 600 Egyptian feet of 307.8mm, 400 cubits of 461.7mm and 220 yards of 839.4mm (33.05″); all valid for the latitude of 'Middle' Egypt.

Why then was the degree of latitude and not longitude chosen for the base of the pyramid, especially since the stadium of latitude is preserved in the apothem? Probably because since the degree of latitude at the equator has the smallest value of degree available, it relates more closely, using pi, to the actual polar radius.

Chapter 5

Who Invented the Metre?

THE Egyptian cubits and feet, of which examples are to be found on graduated rods in the British Museum had a perhaps surprisingly metric value. The scholars have identified units of one foot = 300mm, cubit of 450mm and royal cubit of 525mm.

These units are the metric equivalents of the geographic units in inches as follows:

3″ palm equivalent = 75mm = 1 palm
6″ hand equivalent = 150mm = 2 palms
12″ foot equivalent = 300mm = 4 palms
18″cubit equivalent = 450mm = 6 palms
21″ royal cubit equivalent = 525mm = 7 palms...
when rolled = 22 palms

The palm of 4 fingers (3″) when cubed was the original unit of volume and when filled with water formed the pound or pint of 16 fluid ounces. One fluid ounce was 4 cubic fingers and 1 cubic finger, 4 drams.

A pint was therefore 4 x 4 x 4 = 64 cubic fingers and a cubic foot, 64 pints or 8 gallons of 8 pints.

This system was later adopted by the Greeks, who divided the foot not into 12 'inches', but into 16 'digits'. Two digits made a knuckle and 4 digits a palm. Two palms made a 'lick' of 8 digits whose cube was a gallon. The advantage of dividing the foot into 16 was that its cube could be more readily halved and quartered as a unit of volume.

The cubic foot of water then, not only contained 64 pints but actually weighed 64lbs. (Compare to the metric system where 1 cubic centimetre of distilled water weighs 1 gram – a cube of 10cms contains 1 litre and weighs 1 kilo.)

As a unit of capacity for wheat measure, the cubic foot was later taken by the Greeks as 60 Troy pints or livres, which was however, similar to the ancient Mesopotamian talent of 60 minas.

An attempt was made to recover the original standard in England in 1878 when the gallon was defined as 10lb of water, hence 1 English pint = 20 fl.ozs; the unfortunate result was the English foot became an awkward 6.2 gallons or 62.137lbs. The English hand, used today for measuring horses, came to be a unit in the Greek style, but of 4 inches (100mm) instead of digits.

So to an early Egyptian, 4 fingers made a palm, 4 palms a foot, 6 palms a cubit and 7 palms a royal cubit of 28 fingers. They may not have thought in terms of the metre and millimetre but their units were metric for the simple reason that they had the same root as the metre – the circumference of the Earth.

Eratosthenes, a Greek living in Alexandria around 235BC, is generally credited with the first accurate measurement of the Earth's circumference which he is said to have based on observations of the shadow of a gnomon at the summer solstice. According to the story, he considered the distance between Alexandria and Scyene to be a 50th part of the circumference and by employing the professional Egyptian pacers, found the distance to be 5,000 stadia. This gave a circumference of 250,000 stadia or 25,000 miles.

In order to conform to the above statement, each 'mile' would have to be…..

$$\frac{40.000.000 \text{metres}}{25,000} = 1600 \text{metres}$$

At 1,000 paces to the mile, each pace must be 1600mm and each step 800mm.

The metre in many minds has become a fixedly decimal concept, but with a mile of 1600 metres and a pace of 1600mm, we can envisage a 'metric foot' of 400mm and a 'metric hand' of 100mm so that
4 palms of 75mm make an Egyptian short foot of 300mm and
4 hands of 100mm make a metric or great foot of 400mm.

Bearing in mind that the metre seems to have existed long before it was officially 'invented' and also that in this narrative we are merely trying to follow a path someone else may have taken thousands of years before our time, consider now how they might have approached the same problem.

It would appear that all the units of measurement have common and highly organised origins and that at one time someone executed a detailed and accurate survey of the planet. Only isolated fragments of these measuring systems have survived of which the metric system as described here may be considered an example.

4 metres
9
8
7
6
5
4
3
2
1
3 metres
9
8
7
6
5
4
3
2
1
2 metres
9
8
7
6
5
4
3
2
1
1 metre
9
8
7
6
5
4
3
2
1 hand

*A metric rod
of 4 metres*

Today we use the most sophisticated and accurate equipment which we can devise but which has evolved according to our practical requirements. For example, to survey a terrain we mount a theodolite on a tripod and read from a metric staff, built for convenience in three telescopic sections and extending to four metres graduated in 'hands' of 100mm.

To find distance, the method is this; the surveyor sets up the theodolite on his tripod while his assistant goes out to the required position. He extends the staff and stands behind it, holding it as steady as possible. The surveyor now reads the number of 'hands' appearing in his theodolite between two calibrated lines and multiplies these by ten to find the distance in metres. The further away the staff is, the smaller it appears and the more difficult it is to count the 'hands' and recognise the metre positions on the staff.

The Egyptian system of writing uses a hieroglyphic symbol to represent a picture. Over the years, these symbols have become so stylised that what was originally intended may no longer be clear because the symbol has been incorporated into the common language. If we go back to the beginnings of Egyptian history, the Deities are usually shown carrying certain 'insignia' relative to their status. One such symbol has come to be known as "the key of life" – the cross with the looped handle. Now if this had its origins in a practical piece of equipment, I wonder what it would be?

The god, Ptah

It is very often shown grasped in a fashion very similar to the text-book method of holding the handle (which it resembles) of a surveying chain, the cross part being the exact point where the measurement begins and consisting perhaps of a hollow tube through which a pin may be driven into the ground. The Egyptian god, Ptah, from the ancient capital of Memphis was held to be the supreme architect of the heavens. Now consider the divine symbols he is holding.

Note that he has two crosses or handles (one for each end of the chain?)

The lighthouse contraption – the Egyptian symbol for stability – could be interpreted as the surveyor's staff – a telescopic device in four sections shown in the closed position. Now if the metre was used in conjunction with such an instrument, the staff would be 4 metres long (see diagram) and each metre clearly marked by the projecting 'flags'. It would be graduated in metric 'hands' of 100mm (as is the practice today) but would also be 10 of our metric feet of 400mm.

In the circumference of the globe then, there are 40,000,000 metres, 10,000,000 metric rods and 25,000 metric 'miles'.

When Napoleon Bonaparte's engineers surveyed the Great Pyramid during their invasion of Egypt, they found to their surprise that the pyramid stood on a meridian which exactly bisected the Nile delta. The pyramid was oriented to true north and its diagonals extended to the extreme corners of the delta, which could be neatly enclosed within an arc struck with the pyramid at its centre. Some authors quote that the pyramid is therefore placed on the central meridian of Egypt., midway between the official eastern and western boundaries.

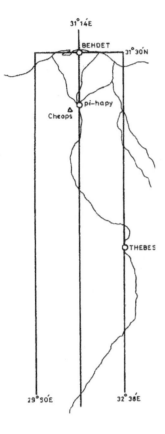

Steccini, in "Secrets of the Great Pyramid" has reconstructed the axes of Egypt as 29° 50′E and 32° 38′E, with one central meridian running from Behdet through Pi-hapy on 31° 14′E. If we look up the Giza plateau on a large-scale map, we would find that it is actually located about 31° 08′E, i.e. about 6 minutes west of the central meridian. Another interesting point about Steccini's eastern meridian axis is that although it passes through the sacred site at Thebes, if it were a boundary, it apparently excludes the temples at Karnak and Luxor on the east bank of the Nile south of Thebes including the famous observatory well at Scyene.

Why then is the greatest architectural masterpiece of the ancient Egyptian world, the Great Pyramid, not situated on the

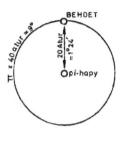

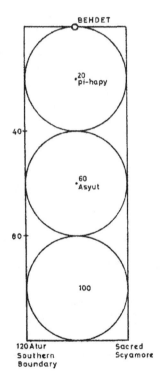

Egyptian prime meridian? Looking at a map of the Delta, and drawing meridians north through Cheops and Pi-Hapy respectively, it would be hard to say which of them more fairly bisected the delta. But then, do we know that the delta had the same shape 5,000 years ago that it has today? In fact the case seems to be that Pi-Hapy lies on the central meridian of Egypt, aligned to the course of the Nile, while Cheops' pyramid was built on a unique meridian aligned to the geography of the delta.

Pi-Hapy was on the banks of the Nile at a point where it divides and fans out through the delta. The records in the temple at Thebes give the northernmost point in Egypt as Behdet at 31° 30′N and the distance from Behdet to Pi-Hapy as 20 atur. The atur was a unit of 15,000 royal cubits. Since Pi-Hapy was at 30° 04'N, the atur was 4.2 minutes of latitude; the distance from Behdet to Pi-Hapy is 1° 24' of latitude and from Pi-Hapy to the eastern or western axis, 1° 24' of longitude.

With a name like Pi-Hapy, the temptation to make Pi-Hapy the centre of a circle with Behdet on its circumference is irresistible.

The perimeter of this circle is therefore pi x 40 atur which in a more recognisable form is exactly nine degrees.

Three such circles placed end to end would give Egypt a length of 120 atur and indeed the official southern boundary was at one time at a place called "sacred sycamore" and correspondingly, 120 atur from Behdet.

Four circles end to end would give an absolute length to Egypt of 160 atur and take us down into Nubia, an area which was exploited for its gold deposits under the Shepherd Kings of the Middle Kingdom. Here at Soleb, a magnificent temple was built by Amenhotep III. Like those at Karnak, Luxor and Thebes, it was in honour of the god Amen or Amon, who, prior to the rise of Thebes as a political centre had been an obscure god from the desert area to the west, possibly the geographic centre of all Egypt. After Amenhotep III, his son attempted to introduce a new religion in worship of the sun disc, the Aten. He changed his name from Amenhotep IV to Akenaten and built his city and political centre about 150 miles north of Thebes, where he retired with his beautiful wife, Nefertitti. After his death, all traces of his activities were obliterated and the old religion reverted to again; Amon found favour again when the 10 years old boy king changed his name back from Tutankaten to Tutankamun.

The builders of the megalithic stone rings devised ellipses with the aim of having both the diameter and the circumference of the ring as whole numbers. Can it be that the Egyptians had the same objective, simply by using geographic units for the perimeter and re-defining the diameter in terms of Atur?

To explain further, say we take the great circle of the Earth with a circumference of 360 degrees. Because of the value of pi, the diameter becomes the awkward number of 114.591 degrees. To get over this obstacle, we retain 360 degrees for the perimeter, but re-define the diameter in a new unit. Here is ArTUR's Round Table which sits 1600 knights, only instead of calling them knights we will call them atur in honour of the once and future king. The diameter is divided into 1600 Atur and the atur is further divided into 15,000 royal cubits resulting in a diameter of 24,000,000 royal cubits of 20.6265″

$$\frac{360°}{\Pi} = 114.591°$$
$$= 114.591° \times 60 \text{ miles} \times 6,000\text{ft} \times 12″$$
$$= 495,035,530″ \qquad = \frac{496,035,530″}{24,000,000} = \frac{20.6265″}{\text{royal cubit}}$$

From a royal cubit of 20.6265″ as the diagonal of a square, we have a side of 1 remen of 14.5851″ which, as a 5,000th part of a minute of latitude computes back to a mean figure for a minute of latitude of 6077.13ft (compare to today's figure of 6076.8884ft).

Today we accept a nautical mile as a round figure of 6080ft for general use on the globe's surface. So we could infer that whoever requires to use a mean figure for a degree of arc has a global interest rather than a local one, where we are forever calculating local values for a minute of latitude.

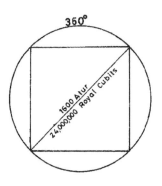

The graticule system of latitude and longitude is such that if we wished to set out a large square on the Earth's surface, then at the latitude of Egypt for example, it would take 6 minutes of longitude to equal 5 minutes of latitude and even then, the results would be only an approximation.

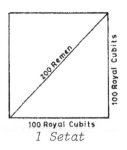

1 Setat

The system of remen and royal cubits would seem to offer the greater advantage that a perfect square can be constructed around any geodetic point.

In practical terms this means that to set out an allocation of 1 setat (a square of 100 x 100 royal cubits) we need only stretch out a cord of 200 remen and intersect two arcs of 100 royal cubits. It is an old saying that "there is nothing new under the sun" and the ratio of 1 remen to 1 royal cubit is to the square root of 2 – exactly the same as the modern "International Standard" metric paper ratios!

The modern unit for measuring land is the hectare and further compares to the setat in that both are a square of 100x 100 units. Thus the setat is 100 x 100 royal cubits and the hectare, a square of 100 x 100 metres.

It is said that when the gods created the world, they began by making Egypt perfect. The four circles of 40 atur end to end form a corridor on the Nile and give a maximum length to Egypt of 160 atur. These circles in turn, could be enclosed in one great circle of perimeter 36° encompassing the whole of Egypt so that the great circle of Egypt is a tenth that of the globe.

Taking the length of Egypt as the diameter of a 36° circle gives a central geodetic point (C1) on the meridian axis between the El Kharga oasis and the city of Thebes. The exact location of this central point will depend on whether we consider the length of Egypt as $\frac{36°}{\pi}$ and calculate in degrees of arc, or take the diameter as 160 atur of 2,4000,000 royal cubits, ascribe a value to the royal

cubit and convert back to degrees using the mean
value of a degree of latitude in Egypt.

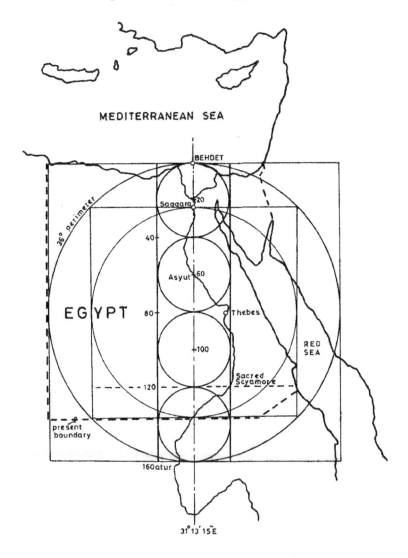

Calculating in degrees of arc gives a central parallel at 25° 46'N, and it is 1,000,000 geographic

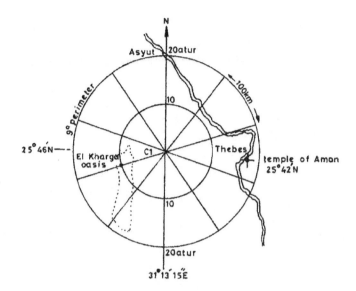

cubits of 450mm north of here that the first stepped pyramid was constructed at Saqqara. Although Saqqara has largely been overshadowed by the later Cheops pyramid, it is Saqqara that is the geodetic pyramid of all Egypt, in fact, its Arabic name of Harem el Modarrggeh even means the pyramid of degrees.

Saqqara was on the original central meridian axis of Egypt, which I would estimate as 31° 13' 15"E and from Saqqara, an arc of 200km radius would enclose the delta in a segment of 90°. Saqqara was where Upper Egypt of the Nile met Lower Egypt of the Delta and the site is one seventh of the length of Egypt from the northern boundary at Behdet.

Numerous tomb complexes were built here, dating back to as early as 3,000BC.

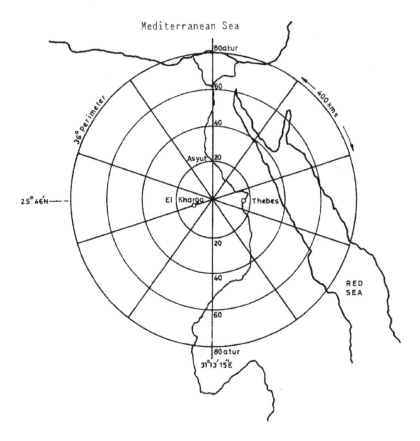

The stepped pyramid of Saqqara was cleverly designed by Imhotep to include a system of internal buttresses which gave it strength and stability enabling it to outlast many of the later pyramids. The pyramid of Meidum followed Saqqara, and could also exert claims to enclose the Delta in a segment of arc, this time with a radius of 250kms. It is virtually on the same meridian as Cheops, but it is

Cheops pyramid itself which has the best claim to domination of the delta, this time with a radius of 100 geographic miles and a segment of 100° of arc.

The central geodetic point C1 at El Kharga suggests that this geodetic system was designed to be the core of a series of spherical projections which could be computed in degrees or atur radiating out from the centre.

All Egypt can thus be enclosed in a radius of 80 atur (36° perimeter) and each segment of arc becomes 400kms on the circumference. For degrees we can also read kilometres since a radius of 90° is at the same time 10,000kms. When we expand this spherical system to include the whole world, it is the diameter which is given a value in degrees (or kms) and this time the circumference is given a value in atur. Imagine you are standing on the North Pole looking down to the equator. You know the distance is 90° or 10,000kms around the sphere so this distance has to be 'swung up' to your own horizontal plane.

The radius in this projection thus becomes 90° or 10,000kms and the circumference 120,000,000 royal cubits or 8,000atur.

We now have to give the radius a mean figure for a minute of arc in order to calculate the value of a royal cubit on the circumference .... i.e.

$$\frac{90° \times 60\text{nm of } 6077.13\text{ft} \times 2 \times \text{pi}}{120,000,000 \text{ royal cubits}} = 20.619'' \text{ royal cubit}$$

and corresponding
remen of 14.5799″

This cubit of 20.619″ is none other than that found in the south side of the Great Pyramid since 400 cubits = 9072.4″ and Cole's survey found this side to be 9072.99″, suggesting a royal cubit of 20.62″ and remen of 14.58″.

With a radius of 90° or 10,000kms, we can choose between radiating 'parallels' at intervals arranged sexagesimally in degrees, or decimally in kilometres. Similarly the circumference can be divided into 8 divisions of 1,000 atur, or 12 divisions of 10,000,000 royal cubits.

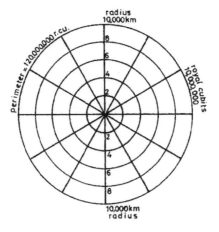

We can also cross the two systems to give a radius of 10,000kms and divisions of 10,000,000 royal cubits!

The famous 'Piri Reis' map, drawn by a Turkish admiral in the 16th century was compiled from such a projection as this. The surviving portion of it shows the coastlines of South America and N.W.Africa much as they appear here, with radiating 'spokes' pointing to a centre in Egypt.

Inaccuracies such as the wrong position of islands in the Caribbean were probably due to the admiral's own revision, when he may have tried to 'update' the map which was also given a system of parallel horizontal and vertical lines suggesting latitude and longitude.

THE WORLD AS A HEMISPHERE

*oblique azimuthal equidistant projection
centred on the great pyramid*

A section of the Piri Reis map along the coast of Africa was examined by the author and found to be absolutely accurate at intervals or 'fixes' of 5°. This suggests that the data had originally been obtained by sailing south along the coast to each 5th parallel, then turning east until land was sighted. The longitude was then reckoned and recorded to be plotted back at the survey base. Joining the points gave the shape of the land and 'infill' irregularities were the result of the imagination of the cartographer of the day.

The sarcophagus of Senostris III

The sarcophagus of the 12th dynasty king, Senostris III may provide an insight to the second geodetic system of Egypt. The cathedral-like structure to the left of the king, as the key to the mapping system of Upper and Lower Egypt, would suggest that a conical projection was used for the Delta, and a transverse cylindrical projection for Upper Egypt. Cylinder seals are quite common artefacts from Egypt and Babylonia and a cylindrical projection the simplest and most obvious for the narrow rectangle of cultivated Egypt. The length of the cylinder is nine degrees so the required cylinder would have a circumference of nine degrees – the same as the circles previously described.

Of the three parallels at the head of the rectangle, the Giza plateau with Cheops pyramid is on the central parallel and the pyramid marks the meridian axis of the delta. The meridian axis of all Egypt passes through Pi-Hapy and intersects the Nile at Asyut on the geodetic parallel of 'middle' Egypt when Egypt has a length of 120 atur.

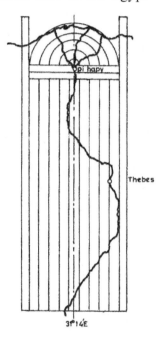

The central, eastern and western axes of Egypt can be seen as three standard meridians, with the central meridian 6' east of the pyramid and the eastern axis passing through the new geodetic centre at Thebes.

This system allows degrees of latitude and longitude to be used in place of the earlier radiating Atur. 20 atur was 1.4324° of arc, but using lat and long, we have to adopt a value of arc in round numbers ie 1.4°. This clears up the mystery of why there were two geodetic points at Pi-Hapy. One was at 30° 04′N, 31° 13′ 15″E on the banks of the Nile and 1.4324° south of Behdet; the other was

at Kher-aha, 30° 06N, 31° 14′E and correspondingly 1.4° south of Behdet.

Thebes was established according to the second
system of Egypt when the system of latitude and
longitude was brought to the fore. The temple of
Amon was built 2/7ths of the distance from the
equator to the pole and 1.4324°E of the central axis.

The rectangle is organised into 9 columns of 24′
of longitude each comprising 4 bands of 6′. The
width of the complete inner rectangle is 216 minutes
or 3.6 degrees of longitude so that at Cheops, it is a
100th part of the 30th parallel. Now this may well
indicate that we are on the right track since Louis
Charpentier diagnosed the cubit of the cathedral at
Chartres to be derived from a 100,000 part of the
degree of longitude in the vicinity of the cathedral.

For the total width of the rectangle we must add
in the two narrower 'flanking' columns each of 3 x
6′ so that the overall width becomes 252 minutes of
longitude...but what is the value of a minute of
longitude?

At Thebes, 60 minutes or 1 degree of longitude
equals 100kms while near Cheops pyramid, at the
geodetically significant 30th parallel, each minute of
longitude corresponds to one English statute mile.

At Alexandria however, near the ancient Egyptian
town of Canopus, each minute of longitude could be
called 10 Egyptian 'stades' of 158.73 metres
because on this parallel, 252 minutes of longitude
i.e. the width of the sarcophagus grid equals a 100th
part of the Earth's circumference!

Now let us suppose that the Once and Future King wishes to find the distance between two of his cities. He orders a special chariot to be made with the intention of counting the revolutions of the wheels. His carpenter however, is but a simple fellow and cannot understand how to construct the necessary wheel with the diameter a funny number so that the perimeter will measure in geographic units. The king calls in Merlin, who provides the carpenter with a special rod whose length is a cubit and a palm - 21″. The carpenter can now use the rod as a gauge for the diameter of the wheel and accordingly builds the chariot.

To Perceval, the task of making the journey is given. He sets out, counting the revolutions as he goes along. After 120 revolutions he would have covered one English furlong and 8 furlongs later, a Statute mile. The wheels unfortunately were a bit on the small side and went round so fast that our poor knight fell asleep, so for the return journey, he ordered another chariot this time with a radius of 21″ and a diameter of 2 grail cubits. Now Perceval has only to count 60 revolutions for his furlong but again lost count of the furlongs and revolutions (480) for his mile.

The king orders Launcelot, his best knight, to make the trip. This time Merlin counsels a diameter of 4 grail cubits (7 English feet) for the special cart and after 240 revolutions, Launcelot has successfully measured the king's Statute mile.

Merlin, like all great geniuses was by nature somewhat absent minded and after the wheels had been constructed according to the grail cubits, he simply dismissed the subject and forgot to ask back the rod engraved with these special cubits. The carpenter was naturally pleased to have been given a 'royal' cubit and it was preserved in his family for many generations. Once the great king and his magician counsellor had begun to recede into distant memory, this cubit came into the possession of a reigning king who decreed that, since it had been given them by a great authority, it ought to become the official cubit of the realm. Unaware that this special cubit was designed to be used with as the diameter or radius of a wheel, this unwise king devised miles and stadia based on straightforward multiples of the Royal cubit.

The Grail cubit was a geographic cubit of 6 palms of 3″ plus an extra palm of 3″ making 7palms or 21″ all told. When rolled as a wheel it measured out 22 palms or a double 33″ cubit i.e. 66″. This unit of 66″ was known in ancient Sumeria and divided into 100 shusi. Three revolutions gave a 'pole' of which 40 made the furlong. When the wheel is 7ft or 4 grail cubits in diameter, it rolls out 22ft and three revolutions measure the old English chain of 22 yards or 66ft (60 Sumerian feet or 1200 shusi): 240 revolutions give the statute mile.

When Peter the Great revised the Russian linear units, he reduced them slightly to make the sajen equal to exactly 7 English feet. The sajen was then divided into 3 arshen of 28″ and 6 fuss of 14″.

On the other side of the channel to Arthur's domains, Charlemagne might have been using a carriage with wheels of the pre-metric unit the toise in diameter. The toise was divided into 6 pieds, 72 pouces or 864 lignes and was an apparently illogical 6.39ft in length. When rolled as a carriage wheel, it measures out 20ft; 3 revolutions give the schonia of 60ft and 30 revolutions the stadium of 600ft.

We can now reconsider Eratosthenes statement that the circumference of the Earth is 250,000 stadia based on the 50th part of the meridian being a paced distance of 5,000 stadia.

The stadium here is usually presumed to be that native to the pacers and is considered by some to be a short unit of 157.7 metres consisting of 300 royal cubits of 525mm. Now this unit was devised hundreds of years before the time of Eratosthenes and its origins and purpose had probably been long forgotten. It should never have been used for a linear pace or step for which purpose it is far too short to be comfortable, just as a metre is too great a step for the average marching man. It was designed to be the diameter of a measuring wheel giving a unit in the tradition of the furlong, 120 revolutions x 8 to the mile.

Before judging Eratosthenes' figure, we must bear in mind that he was supposedly measuring along a meridian from Alexandria to Scyene and as the Earth bulges at the equator, his value should be related to the Polar circumference and not to the larger equatorial circumference.....

Let us say the king's surveyor had a chariot built with wheels of diameter according to the Egyptian royal cubit of 525mm. After the fashion already described, his mile would be 525mm x pi x 120 x 8 = 1583.36 metres and his stadium a tenth of that,

158.33 metres. He can now find the circumference in two ways, first by multiplying his miles by 252 x 100 or secondly by allowing 70 of his miles to a degree x 360. Both methods give a circumference of 24,793 statute miles (39,900,300metres) which is 25 miles short of the actual polar circumference of 24,818 statute miles (British Astronomical Association Handbook).

That is the rational approach. Now try the irrational approach by stating the equation backwards!

Begin by making the circumference the irrational number

3141592653pi

(half-inches)*

divide by   2 for inches

360 for degrees

70 for miles

8 for furlongs

120 for perimeter of wheel

pi for diameter of wheel

= 20.6679″

= <u>525mm royal cubit</u>

*See chapter 12 for full account of pi (half-inches) as circumference of sphere.

If instead of using pi 3141592653, we substitute the figure of 40,000,000 metres we find that the same equation gives

40,000,000 metres

divide by 360 for degrees
70 for miles
8 for furlongs
120 for perimeter of wheel
pi for diameter of wheel
= 526.306mm royal cubit

and a correct 'stadium' of 158.73 metres at 252,000 stades for the circumference.

These figures assume of course, that we are dealing with a perfect sphere, and the actual value of royal cubit by this method will depend on the value we attribute to the circumference e.g. a mean circumference of 40,001,200 metres (using a geographic mile of 6075.8ft) gives a royal cubit of 526.3231mm, which is the value found by Steccini for the cubit of the coffer related to volume.

It should now be apparent to the reader that Eratosthenes was merely re-issuing and juggling with the old Egyptian figures, since unknown to him, not only is the distance form Alexandria to Scyene a 50th part of the meridian, but at the unique parallel of Alexandria (Canopus), 252 minutes of longitude equal a 100th part of the Earth's circumference.

Eratosthenes later got back on the right track when he revised his estimate to 252,000 stadia in order to allow 700 stadia to the degree.

Ptolemy undid the good work by using a Royal Egyptian Stadium of 400 royal cubits of 525mm and allowing 500 such stades of 210 metres to the degree, giving a less accurate circumference of 180,000 Royal Egyptian Stades or 18,000 miles. This was to deceive a great number of early geographers who wrongly assumed him to have been using 'Greek' or geographic units.

Chapter 6

Geometry of the Spheres

Glastonbury has strong associations with King Arthur since some say that it is the island of Avalon, sometimes called the island of glass or island of apples, to which Arthur was carried by the ladies in the barge. Indeed, the body of an uncommonly large man was once said to have been discovered by the monks of the abbey in a very deep grave marked by a great cross.

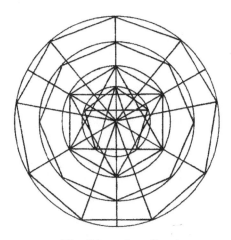

The Glastonbury Bowl

It is to Glastonbury that Joseph of Arimathea first came and according to tradition, drove his staff into the ground, whereby the staff took root and turned itself into the Holy Thorn Tree. Here Joseph brought the sacred cruets and with his twelve companions founded the first church on a grant of land consisting of twelve hides.

To this day a thorn tree still grows on the site, to flower each Christmas in the garden next to the Chalice well.

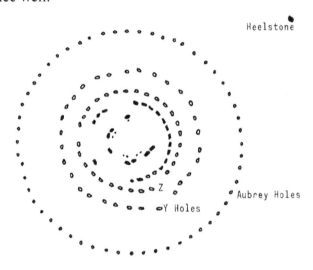

Stones and Holes at Stonehenge

A surviving artefact from the ancient settlement is the Glastonbury Bowl, now in the British Museum. Engraved on the base of the bowl is the geometry we can now identify with Kepler as the 'Geometry of the Spheres'.

Each circle has one less division than its predecessor ending in this case, with the pentagram in the centre.

I believe it was Inigo Jones who, after his survey for King James I, first recognised that a hexagon could be imposed on the inner stones at Stonehenge.

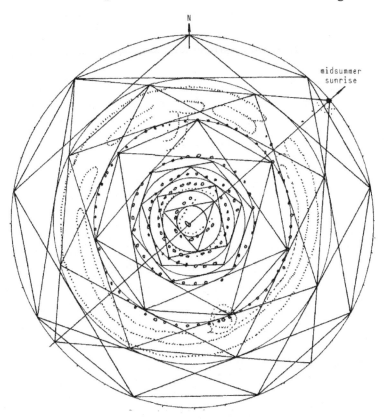

Geometry of the Spheres at Stonehenge

This hexagon may be part of a far greater integrated geometry. If a circle is drawn from the centre, with the heelstone on the perimeter, then this circle becomes the outermost circle of the 'geometry of the spheres'. When divided into nine, it encloses a lesser circle which is divided into eight, which in turn encloses the circle of Aubrey holes which is divided into seven and so on.

The mysterious aspects of Stonehenge lend credibility to the notion that it was a Druid temple and used for some sort of barbaric religious rites. Geoffrey of Monmouth in his "History of the Kings of Britain" gives the credit for its building to the wizard Merlin who had been asked to suggest a burial memorial for the Britons who had been slain by the Saxon leader, Hengst. The stones had been erected in Ireland by a race of giants who had originally brought them from deepest Africa. They were to be used for their healing powers so that when one felt ill, one should bathe in water which had been poured over the stones. Only the powerful Merlin with his magic could overcome the difficulty of transporting these massive stones from Ireland and this he did easily by magically flying them over the sea.

It seems possible that the Bluestones formed part of a circle standing, not in Ireland, but in Wales. These stones came from a quarry in the Prescelly Mountains and were brought over and set up in a double ring during the second construction phase of Stonehenge. In the earliest stage at Stonehenge the builders excavated a circular ditch and built up a 6ft high embankment on the inside, about 20ft wide and 320ft in diameter. The 56 'Aubrey' holes, which may have contained upright posts, form a circle within the embankment.

With the exception of the bluestones, most of the other stones at Stonehenge were quarried comparatively nearby, at Marlborough Downs. The gigantic heelstone came from Marlborough, as did the other sarsen stones which, together with the bluestones, were re-arranged into a single circle and horseshoe arrangement in the third and final building stage.

As a result of thorough analysis by Professor Alexander Thom, verified by other experts in mensuration and astronomy, it has been shown that most of the megalithic circles, rings or menhirs contain complex geometrical arrangements and are constructed on solar, lunar or astronomical alignments.

Consider that for half the year the sun appears to travel northwards and for the other half, southwards, thus setting each day at a slightly different point on the horizon. An observer from a fixed point could mark these extremities of the sun's travels with a standing stone, the half-way point between these two stones being the time of the equinoxes. This simple calendar would warn him of the approach of the winter and summer solstices as the sun drew nearer the outer markers. From the centre of Stonehenge, the Heelstone marks the point where the sun will rise on Midsummer's Day.

When used in this manner, the tall standing menhir becomes the foresight for an alignment; the larger and further away it is, the more accurate the observation. The largest surviving menhir is that of Er Grah at Quiberon in Brittany. This huge 60ft stone could be seen from 10 miles away and may have been used in conjunction with the rows of stones at nearby Carnac. A sharply defined mountain peak could also be used in a similar fashion providing an excellent ready-made foresight;

the backsight or marker posts or stones being placed at the time of observation.

Megalithic man thus provided himself with an accurate calendar and made observations of the sun, moon and stars over a continuous period of thousands of years. With his lunar observations, not only was he able to plot the major and minor standstills of the moon when it reached the end of its travels north and south, but he was also able to determine the amount of the almost imperceptible 'wobble' which is the key to predicting eclipses.

To Professor Thom goes the credit for recognising the existence of a standard unit of length in the stone circles – the megalithic yard – and also for realising the astronomical and geometrical significance of the circles and rings. Thom surveyed over 600 sites in Britain and France and it was only as the work progressed that he became aware of the extreme accuracy required to survey these sites in order to match the accuracy with which they were set out. Just as Petri set out stations on the plateau around the Great Pyramid, the only way to absolutely determine the accuracy of the Stonehenge alignments is to set out surveying stations far into the surrounding landscape.

Thom established the existence of a megalithic yard of 2.72ft and a 2½ times multiple, the megalithic rod of 6.8ft. Thom suggested that this megalithic yard was originally carried around as a rod or stick, the word yard meaning stick and with equivalents such as the Spanish vara from Burgos of 2.766ft. He also discovered a complex mathematical geometry within the circles and flattened rings, often derived from an arrangement of Pythagorean (whole number) right angled triangles.

At Avebury, the largest of the stone rings, the design is conceived around a 3,4,5 triangle in units of 25my so that the ultimate numbers are multiples of 5 or 10.

Any circle whose diameter is 10 units will have a circumference of pi units and megalithic man seemed to have a dread fear of producing a circle whose perimeter was an awkward number of units. To put it another way, he wanted both the diameter and the circumference to be a whole number of units so he invented a system of 'flattening' the rings to produce the result he wanted.

It has long been recognised that many of the churches and cathedrals in Britain were built upon formerly pagan religious sites. The object was not to alienate the old worshippers but to absorb them into the new religion, even to the extent as in France, where a church was built around a standing menhir.

When the builders replaced an ancient religious site with a church, or divined the location for themselves, we cannot be certain that they were conscious of an underlying plan, but by placing monuments on these old sites, they automatically adopted the ancient pattern.

Alfred Watkins, whilst out riding, had a vision. He could see the whole country covered in a network of straight lines joining all the sites of antiquity. The "Old Straight Track" was born. Ley hunters claim that the whole country is covered with large scale geometrical patterns. From alignments, they can predict where to find stones or markers and provided that the stone has not been removed or destroyed, they are usually right.

The number of stones remaining is enormous, yet it can only be a fraction of what once existed. Over the years the stones have been removed, particularly by farmers, who as at Avebury, even devised a special method to destroy them by casting them into a fiery pit and then dousing them with cold water. At Carnac, in France, the church authorities would ensure that a stone was religiously destroyed on feast days.

The placing of a stone has something in common with a cross.

The original cross was an upright stake or stone and a good example can be seen in Ely cathedral. This is St. Ovin's Cross which was removed from Haddenham where it was last used as a mounting block, and taken to the cathedral for preservation. The cross was prob-ably found at

St. Ovin's Cross

cross roads, where ley lines meet. Long before the Christian era we find the True cross or Celtic cross, with equal length arms set upon a circle. Join the points of the cross and you have the circle squared.

Meriden is a small village five miles NW of Coventry. It has an ancient stone cross and according to local legend is traditionally the centre of England. If we look at the figure, a circle centred on Meriden neatly contains the whole of England and a smaller circle passes through Glastonbury and Bury St. Edmunds, both known to be on the longest alignment 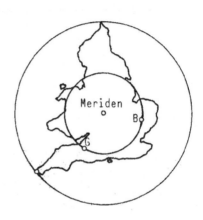 in southern England and formerly two of the most powerful (Benedictine) abbeys in Britain.

If a ley hunter can predict where to find a stone, or continuation of a geometrical pattern, it follows that these markers must have been laid out according to a strict geometrical survey. As these stones extend the length and breadth of the British Isles, then fixed reference points must have been established in accordance with survey practice. The construction of a massive hill such as Silbury could serve a double function. By placing a pole on its summit it could act as an astronomical calculator or sundial. It could also be used as a trig reference point as could Glastonbury Tor or any other so called 'castle' mound.

The system of triangulation in field surveying works on the principle that once you have measured the length of your base line, all the other survey points can be established by measuring the angles and calculating the distance, between intervisible stations. Where no natural station occurs, such as a hillock, it would be necessary to build an elevated position such as a mound. The countryside is covered with ancient mounds which even today are sometimes used by the Ordnance Survey as Trig points for our modern maps although our survey only goes back some 150 years. Naturally not every mound was necessarily a trig mound, but the passing of time telescopes them all into the same bracket and they are all 'castle hills' to the average onlooker.

One such intriguing mound is known as Farley Mount in Hampshire, not far from Winchester. The origins of this mound go well back before the Saxon era and it is one of the few mounds in Hampshire not to have been utilised by the Saxons with perhaps a settlement nearby and a church on the top as at Corhampton and Cheriton. Elsewhere such as Carisbrooke, Christchurch and Southampton, great mounds were used to support the castle keeps. Farley Mount is surrounded by a ring shaped entrenchment and appears to have been a site sacred to the Celtic peoples of this area who considered such mounds to be the Gods mounds. It is reminiscent of the mounds or high places mentioned in ancient Hebrew history and is surrounded by some of the most ancient roads in Hampshire. These ancient hollow ways are mentioned in the Anglo-Saxon charters as being hollow or old ways, a thousand years ago. Worn

down by the traffic of ages past they are perhaps
those same ways which were, "cut down out of time
and whose foundations were overflown with a
flood".

Farley Mount

In the early part of the nineteenth century, a
member of the local gentry was saved from a nasty
fall by his horse which executed a marvellous leap
across a gully. To commemorate this famous horse,
when it died, he erected the 'horse monument'
which stands out conspicuously atop the ancient
mound

Another interesting site, which is usually labelled
as an iron age hill fort, is that of Wandlebury with
its circular ditch embankment, near Cambridge.
About 14kms to the NE of Wandlebury, the Devils
Dyke follows the alignment of the midwinter sunrise
for a distance of 11,500 metres and about 4km from

Wandlebury, the Fleam Dyke follows roughly the same orientation but with a more pronounced curve.

Both the Devils Dyke and the Fleam Dyke are usually thought to have been defensive works and of Saxon origin due to Roman and post Roman remains found trapped under their embankments.

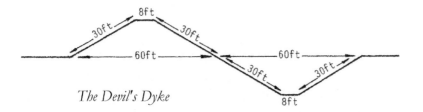

The Devil's Dyke

A section of the Devils Dyke examined by the author suggested no clumsily constructed earthen defence but a clever and meticulously designed embankment such that its sloping side continued into the ditch and the embankment was the exact counterpart of the ditch from which the material had been excavated. The ditch was of 'V' shaped profile with a flat bottom 8ft wide. The overall width of the ditch was 60ft, the length of each sloping side 30ft and the angle of slope 30°; the depth of the ditch and the height of the corresponding bank were accordingly 15ft. The conclusion was that the ditch had been dug out and the bank built up according to a rod or reed of 15ft.

A cross section examined early this century by the Cambridge Antiquarian Society found that the embankment had first been marked out by the topsoil from the ditch and then filled in with the excavated chalk.

A 'Roman' road which runs for a distance of 10kms in a curve almost parallel to the Fleam Dyke was also examined by the Society. It was found to be aligned along a partially levelled vallum of pre-Roman origin, - "it certainly was not a military work and no suggestion can be offered to its purpose."

Today, Wandlebury is an attractive nature reserve, largely overgrown wit shrubbery and trees. The preservation of these trees is a subject of local concern but had we visited the site before the trees were established, what would we have found?

Well, the ring ditch was a perimeter of 900 metres and the outlying embankment approaches a thousand metres in circumference – a scale comparable to Avebury.

The site occupies an elevated position on the Gog Magog hills and from here we would be able to see for miles over the surrounding countryside. On a three dimensional, layer tinted contour map, Wandlebury appears as an island on the edge of a flat basin surrounded by gently rolling hills and its vantage point offers intervisibility to the numerous tumuli usually found on promontories of rising land on the edges of these hills.

To the south-east at a distance of 600 metres, there stands a perfectly conical artificial mound (Wormwood Hill) 50 metres in diameter and to the east at a distance of 1600 metres or 1 statute mile (the same distance as Silbury Hill to Avebury) another overgrown mound, Copley Hill with a base 150metres in diameter – again a similar dimension to Silbury Hill. To the north-east, at a distance of exactly 10,000 metres, the largest mound in the area is Allington Hill, which appears to be an artificial mound with a base 250 metres in diameter built up on a naturally occurring headland.

To the north, we have the 'castle' mound at Cherry Hill, Ely; to the north-west, that of Cambridge and to the south, the 50 metre diameter mound at Elmdonbury. To someone in the vicinity of Wandlebury, the Midwinter Sun would rise from the direction of Bartlow where there is a group of small mounds known as the 'seven sisters' and it would set in the direction of Royston where a similar number of mounds stands on the heath. Royston also boasts a funnel shaped subterranean cave which might possibly have been used to observe the transit of a star.

It is tempting to think of a megalithic ring as a large protractor and the larger the ring, the greater would be the accuracy of our angular measurement. On a ring whose circumference is 21.6 metres, each millimetre on the circumference would be a minute of arc; for each millimetre to equal a second of arc, we would need a ring 1276 metres in circumference – something the size of Avebury!

If we wished to increase our accuracy even further, we could in fact dispense with the ring altogether and build only a section of curved embankment of increased radius.

If the position of some celestial body were marked with a stone, we would have yet another inexplicable avenue similar to the cursus at Stonehenge or the long rows of stones at Carnac, Brittany.

The henge type of circular enclosure, which is common throughout Britain is usually accompanied by a large mound and often there is a dyke or cursus in the nearby area. The key to these mysterious embankments then, may be that they were designed to be viewed across and not down their lengths.

The long rows of stones at Carnac are part of a vast geometrical design on a hardly discernable curve of radius 2,500 megalithic yards (1,000 megalithic rods).

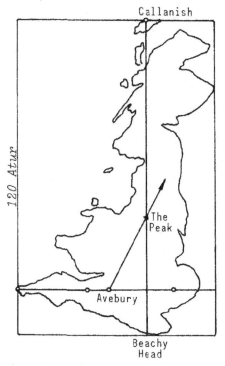

The longest alignment in southern England is generally held to be from St Michael's Mount in Cornwall, to Glastonbury, Avebury and Bury St Edmunds. At right angles to this alignment, we could envisage another long alignment from Callanish through THE PEAK to Beachy Head. This would form the basis for a rectangle which would contain Britain and fix its official dimensions as 80 x 120 atur.

Of course it will be immediately argued that all these straight lines are in fact curves on the surface of the earth, and indeed over a distance, this is so. Yet every map is an attempt to render the curved surface of the globe as a flat projection on paper.

Sometimes it is an advantage to have a projection which shows the parallels and meridians as curves, but more often it is of greater convenience to show them as straight lines at right angles to each other. Mercator's World Map was such a projection, with the upper and lower parallels spaced further apart to compensate for the apparent stretching out of the land masses.

It is a cylindrical projection with the cylinder placed around the earth at the equator. The Earth is then considered to be cut along the meridians, like the segments on an orange, and these meridians are plotted as vertical lines on the cylinder. Because the Earth is basically a sphere, the cylinder could be placed to touch along any meridian or great circle instead of the equator. In the case of a smaller area such as Great Britain, the cylinder is 'rolled' along a standard meridian, 2° west, (note how useful the meridian 1° 54' west passing through The Peak and Avebury might have been) and the projection is known as the Transverse Mercator.

It is also an even greater advantage for the map to have the benefit of a super-imposed grid, where the vertical and horizontal lines form regular squares instead of elongated rectangles. This is sometimes known as an 'artillery' grid because it enables any position on the map to be readily identified by a set of co-ordinates east and north of the zero origin of the map.

Prior to the introduction of the Transverse Mercator projection, each county had been independently surveyed at a scale of 25 inches to the mile on the Cassini projection. A point near the centre of the county was selected as the Origin and the projection based on the meridian passing through this point. Some of the smaller counties were grouped together for this series, but in general, it was impossible to match up the county surveys to form a national map. Before the First World War, a system of two-inch squares had been imposed on the existing one-inch maps for each county so that each square could be identified by a letter from one margin and a number from the other. Improvements in artillery accuracy urged the introduction of a system sub-dividing the squares into hundreds and eventually a national system continuous throughout the entire country.

For Great Britain, the Ordnance Survey began in 1924 to compute a Transverse Mercator projection centred on meridian 2° west and latitude 49° north. This was to form the basis of the new one-inch map and had the advantage of a minimum of distortion with a reasonable uniformity of scale over the entire area.

All Parallels are presented as curves and all Meridians as straight lines ultimately converging at the Pole, but the overlying grid consists of straight lines parallel and at right angles to each other.

Decoding Ezekiel's Temple

Because of the convenience of the decimal metre, this was adopted as the unit for the new grid.

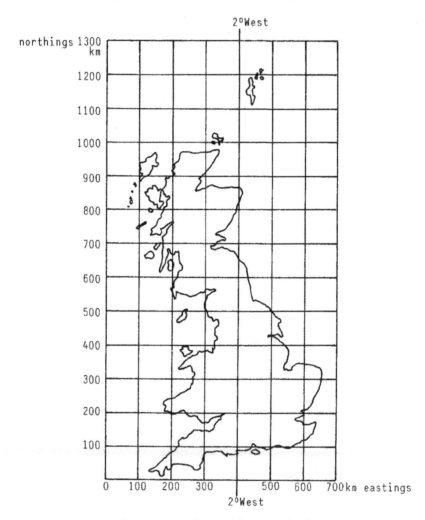

The Ordnance Survey National Grid

In order to give all co-ordinates on the National Grid positive values, a 'false' or zero origin is fixed at a point just south-west of Land's End. The grid forms a rectangle 700 x 1300 kms and is divided primarily into 100km squares. Since the squares to the north of the 1,000km northing could have co-ordinates which are a repetition of those to the south, all square are now given unique identification letter prefixes. The smallest squares drawn on the one-inch map (1:63,360) or the latest 50,000 scale replacement are at 1km intervals.

Each 1km square can be further sub-divided and any position in Great Britain can thus be pin-pointed to the nearest metre by quoting the 100km square prefix followed by two, 5-figure references east and west.

In Britain, triangulation began as a simple device for finding the range of a gunnery target but was quickly developed as a means of surveying and finding the shape of the spheroid. The first British triangulation was begun in 1785 Bt Major-General Roy to determine the difference in longitude between the observatories of Greenwich and Paris and thus the dimensions of the Earth, but with the ultimate objective of providing a general survey of the British Isles.

A base line was first marked out on Hounslow Heath by two army officers and its ends marked by two partially buried cannons. The measurement of the base line is a lengthy and tedious business involving stretching steel tapes across specially prepared tripods set at short intervals apart, but the resultant measurement can have an accuracy as high as one in a million. The accuracy of the triangulation increases in relation to the size of the triangles and for a principal triangulation, sides of upwards of 20 miles are used. This primary triangulation quickly and accurately covers the entire country, but to fill in the local detail secondary and then tertiary triangulations are used, the last having stations at one mile intervals.

The angles are determined by a theodolite, an instrument consisting of a powerful telescope through which a point may be observed and its bearing read off in degrees, minutes and seconds from a graduated circle. The stations have to be well defined and easily seen through the theodolite; powerful electric beacon lamps have been used at night to project a fine beam, of light for the most accurate surveys. Once the survey stations or trig points have been accurately determined, they have to be permanently marked by such a method as setting brass bolts into the roofs of churches, water towers, etc.

Where no convenient building or high point is available, steel observing towers may be erected over the survey point to allow intervisibility to continue over obstructions such as trees.

The principal triangulation of Great Britain continued over many years and finished in 1853. Seven bases were established at sites including Salisbury Plain and Lough Foyle. Observations were made with Ramsden's Great Theodolite having a circle 36° circle. in diameter. Over thirty astronomical observations were made to further determine the accuracy of the survey and help determine the shape of the spheroid.

The second and tertiary triangulations were not made with the same amount of accuracy and the stations were not sufficiently well marked so that by this century many of them had disappeared.

A new survey was commenced using modern methods and the smaller Tavistock theodolite with a 5½ inch circle. The astronomical observations were dispensed with but as some twelve of the original primary survey points were used in re-triangulation, it is in fairly close agreement with the original.

Chapter 7

The Crusade for Jerusalem

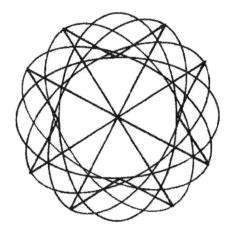

The two centuries following the Norman conquest of England were a time of great religious enthusiasm and expansion in Western Christendom. Many new religious orders were founded, the drive for Jerusalem began and enormous building projects were undertaken too transform the new energy into the timeless monumental architecture of the cathedrals and monastic establishments. The impulsion was kept up through the activities of a few individuals such as Bernard de Fontaine whose Cistern Order founded 356 new houses in twenty-five years. Bernard, Abbe de Clairvaux, visualised a united Europe under his Cistercians. With the additional knowledge gained through the Templars in the east, he was able to suggest to Cretien de Troyes that the Queste du Sainte Graal be undertaken.

The crusades for Jerusalem were preached by Pope Urban II to liberate the Holy Land from the hands of the Saracens and ensure the safety and well being of the Christian pilgrims who wished to worship at the church of St. Sepulchre. In July 1099, the city fell to the Christian knights and the road to Jerusalem was secure. The Holy Land had to be held and defended against the recurrent attacks of the Saracens, so the knights strengthened their positions by building fortified castles and forming themselves into a military order.

The Order of the Knights Templar was founded by Hugh de Payens in 1118 for the protection of the pilgrims and was followed in 1120 by the Knights Hospitallers who were to tend to the wounded and sick, soldiers and pilgrims alike. Both Orders took monastic vows of a particularly severe nature. The

Rule for the Templars was formulated by St. Bernard, who forbade ostentatious displays of gold, silver, finery and luxury and encouraged fasting, asceticism and religious devotion. The Templars established their headquarters on the site of King Solomon's Temple, occupying the palace of Baldwin II and taking for their emblem the design of the Dome of the Rock, which they held to be the Temple of the Lord.

The round churches they built on their return to Europe were closely modelled on this shrine, derived from the church of the Holy Sepulchre.

The site of the Rock is sacred to Muslims, Jews and Christians. It is the site where Abraham offered his son Isaac as a sacrifice to the lord. The arc of the covenant was brought here to be placed in the innermost part of the Temple and it was from this spot that the prophet Mohammed made his night-journey to Heaven.

This site, on Mount Moriah, was bequeathed to Solomon by his father King David along with the resources necessary for the construction of the sacred Temple. And so it came to pass in the 480th year after the children of Israel were came out of the land of Egypt, that Solomon began to build the House of the Lord. By treaty with Hiram, king of Lebanon, he obtained cedar and fir trees, raising a levy of 30,000 men and sending them in relays, 10,000 per month to assist in the felling and transportation. For the timber he paid 20,000 measures of wheat and 20 of pure oil per year as well as ceding 20 cities in the north of the country.

Great and costly stones were made ready for the foundations of the house, prepared away from the site so that neither hammer nor axe nor any tool of iron was heard in the house while it was being built. The length of the house was sixty cubits, the breadth twenty cubits and the height thirty cubits; it had a porch before the temple of the house, twenty cubits in length according to the breadth of the house and ten cubits wide. The house, which had chambers five cubits round about, was finished throughout in beams and planks of cedar, the walls being carved with alternating cherubims and palm trees. The oracle was the most holy place, the destination of the arc of the covenant. It took the form of a cube, 20 x 20 x 20 cubits high. Within the oracle were placed two cherubims carved of olive tree overlaid with gold, ten cubits high, with wings outstretched so that each had a wing, five cubits long, touching a wall while the other wings touched each other in the centre of the House. The oracle was overlaid with gold, as was the whole house, including the floor. The House of the Lord took seven years to build and then Solomon set out to build his own house. This was a structure of 100 x 50 cubits and construction took a further thirteen years. To furnish the accoutrements of the Holy Temple, Solomon sent unto Tyre for Hiram, a master in the working of metal. Amongst the multitude of pieces made for Solomon were two brass pillars eighteen cubits high, which were set up in the porch, also a "molten" sea, hemispherical in shape, ten cubits in diameter, five cubits in height and encompassed by a chord thirty cubits about. This stood on the backs of twelve oxen facing outwards, three looking towards the north, west, south and east respectively.

When all the work was completed, the arc of the covenant containing the two stone tablets of Moses was placed in the oracle beneath the outstretched wings of the cherubims and the House was dedicated to the Lord. Then a cloud descended over the oracle and the Glory of the Lord filled the House of the Lord. To complete the dedication, Solomon made a sacrificial peace offering of 22,000 oxen and 120,000 sheep, finishing things off with a great feast lasting a fortnight.

Solomon prospered greatly, with a fleet at sea bringing home a great traffic in gold, spices and precious stones. In one year, 666 talents of gold came into the country to be beaten into drinking vessels and great shields which he stored in the house. The fame of his wisdom travelled so far that many sought his counsel, adding to his prosperity by bearing precious gifts in exchange for his advice. The great Queen of Sheba sought him out to bear witness for herself the extent of his wisdom.

Now Solomon found a great distraction with his 700 wives and 300 concubines so that he turned away from the Lord. Consequently adversaries were stirred up against him on his frontiers so that eventually, after his death, the city fell to the Babylonians after a long siege in 587BC. Thus Nebuchadnezzar, king of Babylonia took all the treasures form the House of the Lord, cut them up into pieces and carried them off to Babylon, along with a great train of captives comprising all the craftsmen and smiths as well as the king's officers

and wives. The Chaldeans broke down the walls of
the city and burnt the House of the Lord so that

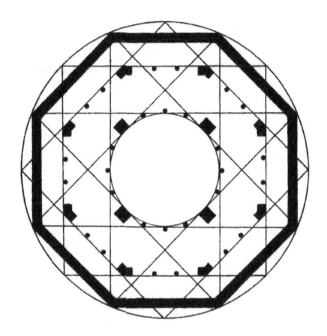

Dome of the Rock

Jerusalem was totally bespoiled, only the poorest
sort of people remaining.

The Temple was to be rebuilt twice in Jerusalem,
that of Herod being burnt by Roman armies under
Titus in AD70 when the land was proclaimed a
Roman province with the title of Syria-Palestine.

In 691, the Khalif Abd al-Malik engaged the
finest craftsmen in the Islamic empire to construct a
shrine over the sacred rock. It was modelled on the
Byzantine Christian churches of the time and has
come to be the oldest surviving example of Muslim
architecture. The golden dome rests on a high drum

set on the top of a flat-roofed, octagonal building. The drum, which has sixteen windows, is supported by an inner circular arrangement of four piers and twelve columns and the weight of the roof is further taken by an octagon of eight piers and sixteen columns of polished marble. Admittance to the shrine is through four huge doors set on each alternate side of the octagonal walls, one facing each of the cardinal points of the compass.

Over the years the Dome has been shaken by earthquakes and destroyed by fire but has always been restored so as to be more beautiful than ever. In 985 it was described as being a most marvellous sight without equal, when, at the dawn, the light of the sun first struck on the cupola and its rays were reflected by the drum. Saladin decorated the inside of the cupola with a tiled inscription and series of medallions and in the early sixteenth century Sulieman II brought beautiful blue tiles from Kasham in Persia, embellishing the exterior according to the Persian style. In modern times the foundations have been reinforced with concrete and the dome sheeted in a special alloy of aluminium and bronze to gleam like gold under the sun's rays.

The Knights of the Temple and those of St. John were organised in three ranks, knights, chaplains and serving brethren. Both Orders had grand Master as head of the Order and became enormously popular over the years, the flower of European chivalry flocking to their standards.

The Templars were recognised by a white robe with a red cross. From their first base in Jerusalem, they later moved to Antioch, Acre and Cyprus. They formed themselves into twelve provinces, Palestine,

Antioch, Tripoli, Greece, Hungary, Portugal, Spain, France, Italy, Germany, the Low Countries and England. They became the international bankers of Europe and their tremendous wealth brought about their downfall. The King of France trumped up charges against them in order to avoid settling his debts and confiscated their properties. Since the Crusades had ended when the Holy Land was retaken by the Saracens, there was technically no more need for the Templars and they were dissolved by Pope Clement V in 1312.

The Knights Hospitallers of the Order of St. John fared a little better. When forced out of the Holy Land, they established themselves on the island of Rhodes which they built up into an island fortress from which they could foray to attack and harass the Arab shipping routes. They continually hoped to re-invade Jerusalem and also planned two campaigns against Egypt but their military power was never strong enough to carry out these projects successfully.

The Knights of St. John wore a black cloak with a white eight-pointed cross which they pledged to defend with their lives. On joining the Order, they were entreated of this cross "that you may love it with all your heart and may your right hand fight in its defence and preservation. Should it ever happen that, in combating against enemies of the Faith, you should retreat and desert the standard of the Cross and take flight, you will be stripped of the true Holy Sign, according to the customs and statutes of the Order, and you will be cut off from our body as an unsound and corrupt member."

The Order had its beginnings in Jerusalem through Gerard de Martigues who had created hospices for the care of sick pilgrims. Around 1120, they were formed into the Order of the Knights of St. John by a French nobleman, Raymond de Puy, who drew up their monastic vows and Rule after the manner of the Augustinians. They quickly expanded into a powerful and rich organisation owning 19,000 lordships and manors by 1240. In England, their priory of St. Johns, Clerkenwell, was the richest monastic establishment in London with fifty comanderies and its Master was the Grand Prior of all England. When they were defeated by Sulieman, he paid tribute to their glorious feats of arms by generously allowing them to leave their island of Rhodes.

For some years they made representations at the courts of Europe trying to negotiate a new home until they were finally given the island of Malta. Once more they built up a magnificent fortress and from its superb anchorages launched their fleet to continue their sport of harassing the Turks by sea. Matters came to a head when the Great Siege of Malta left them undefeated and Sulieman withdrew his forces. The knights continued to build up the splendid Auberges and developed the city named after their first Grand Master, Valletta.

The Cause failed to maintain the popularity of the early days however, and the power of the knights began to decline. The European nobility no longer saw any merit in the re-conquest of Jerusalem and the Order, as a military force, faded from history.

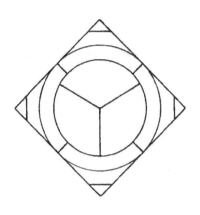

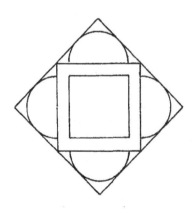

*Floor Designs
at
Ely Cathedral*

"And I John saw the holy city, new Jerusalem, coming down from God out of heaven, prepared as a bride adorned for her husband." This description was preserved in the liturgy for the consecration of a church and identifies the medieval church with the city of God in the Revelation of St. John.

The gothic style of building which was to dominate Europe began with the Abbey of St. Denis on the royal Isle de France. Abbot Sugar was the driving force behind the construction of his abbey but scarcely acknowledged the fact that he was introducing a new form of architecture. The huge size of the building was simply to accommodate the vast crowds of people under one roof yet symbolically, the church had twelve piers in recognition of the twelve apostles and twelve columns for the twelve lesser prophets. Sugar was justly proud of the luminescent quality of the light from his stained glass windows and in the diary of his administration records how these windows were going to direct the spirit of the faithful "by material means towards that which is immaterial".

A certain amount of rivalry existed between the great religious houses; Bernard abhorred all forms of ostentation and in a letter to the Cluniacs, who embellished their churches as richly as possible, Bernard wrote "we suppose it is done for God's honour, but I as a monk ask Tell me ye poor, if ye be poor, what doeth this gold in your sanctuary? – We who have forsaken all precious and beautiful things for Christ's sake, who have counted but dung all things fair to see, soft to the ear, sweet to the smell, pleasant to the touch, whose devotion do we intend to excite by such means? The adoration of fools or the oblations of the simple?"

The Cistercians had begun as a splinter from the Benedictines at the Abbey of Molesine in Burgundy. Dismayed at the disregard for the Rule which prevailed at the House, the abbot Robert and a visiting English monk, Stephen Harding, cleared a wood at Citeaux (Cistercium) and built the parent house of the new order. This was joined by Bernard who later set out with twelve monks and founded the abbey of Clairvaux in the woods at Val d'Abinthe. This pattern of sending out twelve monks under an abbot assisted in the rapid expansion of the Order, and the White Monks – so called from their white cassocks – soon rivalled the long established Benedictines.

The Cistercians adhered to a life of the utmost simplicity and built their abbeys away from the populous areas, on exposed moors, drained marshes or woods which they had cleared.

Whereas the Houses of the Benedictines were largely independent units, the Cluniacs came under the authority of the abbot of Cluny, in Burgundy. It was here that the Order had been founded with the intention of reforming the scattered units of Benedictines and welding them together under one leader, with ideals proposed by St. Benedict of Aniane.

At the time of the Norman Conquest in England, there were fifty Benedictine monasteries in England and this number grew to 245 establishments at the time of the Dissolution. William had sworn to build and dedicate an abbey should he be granted victory and encouraged the Benedictines to settle in England. His request to the Abbot of Cluny to send over twelve monks was initially declined as William had offended the abbot by offering a large sum of money for this purpose; later through the intervention of a mediator, a number of the brethren established their first house at Lewes in 1077. William found it useful that a body of armed men should be provided by the monasteries for the king's service although the monasteries themselves were defined by him as places of sanctuary.

Twelve monks and an abbot were the minimum necessary to constitute a monastery and the word of the abbot was absolute. He was bound to observe the same Rule as his brethren and initially lived with them in common, but in later years the abbot often retired to a private house built within the grounds of the monastery. The monastery issued a dole of meat to the poor and was obliged to provide accommodation for travellers – which could be a serious set-back if the traveller happened to be a noble person with a large retinue.

The monasteries and their churches were not built by the monks themselves but by masons brought in specially for this purpose. Many of the abbeys followed the fixed designs prepared by the parent houses of the Benedictines and Cistercians and building was supervised by the skilled masons from Burgundy and Normandy. When Christchurch Priory in Canterbury was rebuilt in 1124, the masons brought the stone all the way from Caen in Normandy.

Although the focal point of the monastery was the church, containing the huge stone block of the altar where services were performed, life for the monks continued around the cloisters. The other buildings were grouped around this courtyard so that within its sheltered walls, the monks could walk and meditate. Sometimes the monks lived in common rooms or dorters but often they lived a solitary life within their own cells. At Mount Grace Priory, a large number of cells are grouped around three sides of a cloister which is oddly not a true square, but a lozenge, with one side 272ft. It was more usual for the cloisters to be in the form of a true square, that at Castle Acre Priory having sides of 100ft. The chapter house often took the polygonal form, having eight, ten, or twelve sides as at the Cistercian Abbey Doré

In contrast to the occupants of the monasteries, who retreated from the world, the friars went out into the world to preach and give service to the community. Theirs was a life of utter poverty, with no fixed abode but travelling around the countryside living on alms and ministering to the poor. In addition to the Grey Friars of the Order of St. Francis of Assisi, there were the Black Friars, Carmelites and Augustinians. The Augustinian Order of Regular Canons, or Black Canons as they were called, were more individually independent than the members of the other orders. They were not tied to any fixed Rule and attached themselves to the parish churches, mixing more freely with the world at large. Their Abbey of Waltham Cross in Essex was one of the most important in the country when reconstructed as a priory by Henry II in 1177, the church having an estimated length of 480ft. They were not so powerful as the Benedictines, whose manner of building they loosely adopted, yet had 2112 foundations in Britain when they were finally abolished by Henry the Eighth

The monasteries and ecclesiastic establishments in England had become so rich and powerful by Henry's reign that they indirectly challenged his authority on the throne. Henry, who had formerly been dubbed "Defender of the Faith" by the Pope, had a pressing need to obtain a papal dispensation to enable him to marry his dead brother's wife and provide the country with an heir. When this dispensation was not forthcoming he resolved to take the church in England into the royal custody. The orders went out and under the direction of Thomas Cromwell, the monasteries were suppressed, their lands and properties forfeited to the crown. The monastic buildings were either dismantled or razed, setting fire to the roof was the simplest way to recover the lead. The priceless and sacred treasures were melted down for the value of the gold and the illuminated manuscripts, gathered in the libraries over the centuries, added as fuel to the fire..

It has long been thought that many of the great cathedrals and churches embodied the key to a lost science built into their structures. This idea of something more than the great facades, the "storied windows richly deight, casting a dim, religious light" is best summed up in the title of Fulcanelli's enigmatic book "The Mystery of the Cathedrals".

The cathedrals often stood on sites dating from antiquity and in common with the sites of many eastern shrines, they were often distinguished by a well. The cathedral at Winchester stood in danger of collapse owing to the presence of an underground stream and it is largely thanks to the efforts of a diver who placed thousands of bags of cement under the foundations at the turn of the century that it still stands today. Sometimes an abbey would be built directly across a river. Fountains Abbey was built on a drained marsh with four parallel stone tunnels 90 yards long channelling the water beneath the building.

If the site of the cathedral was occupied by a parish church, then that church would be demolished and facilities provided in the cathedral or in another smaller church nearby. At Ely a church dedicated to St. Cross was built for the parishioners on the green adjoining the cathedral but this was later demolished in the reign of Elizabeth I to make way for the Lady Chapel.

The cathedral at Chartres has been thoroughly analysed by Louis Charpentier in "The Mysteries of Chartres Cathedral". He relates how the cathedral is built in strict harmonic dimensions. The height and the breadth of the building are related to the musical scale. Because of the mathematical relationship between notes in music, musical notation could almost be called the language of numbers. Indeed someone even went so far once as to invent an international language which could be spoken, sung, written in notation or played on the piano! Bach was one of the greatest 'mathematical' musicians which is one of the reasons why his music is so fascinating and particularly suited for playing in the cathedral.

Louis Charpentier first became interested in cathedrals when he happened to visit Chartres on the occasion of the summer solstice. At noon, a small circle of light fell on a pre-determined flagstone and his curiosity was aroused; he afterwards proceeded to survey and study the rest of the building.

In order to observe the Chartres phenomenon for myself, and armed with a tape measure to compare English and French measures in the cathedrals, I went to Chartres for the June solstice of 1979.

Before proceeding into the centre of the cathedral, one must cross the labyrinth set into the floor of the nave. According to tradition, the pilgrim must follow the route of the labyrinth in his bare feet before entering the church proper; this is considered a substitute for making the actual pilgrimage to Jerusalem. Today, one might find this task a little difficult as the floor is usually covered with chairs, but they are cleared once a year for the observance of the above rite.

The Labyrinth at Chartres

The centre of the labyrinth was destroyed some time in the past and now consists of a bare stone circle about 62″ in diameter with projecting metal studs. The diameter of the complete labyrinth adds up to 500″ which should be considered as a 1,000,000th part of the Earth's diameter. Remove the 8″ depth of the 'sprocket teeth' and the diameter is now 484″, the same as the interior of the Round Church at Cambridge, which would fit neatly on here.

And how far would the pilgrim walk on his mini-trip to Jerusalem? I followed the path on a photograph using a map-measuring heel, and when I reached the centre, it 'clicked' exactly on 10,000 inches.

One might have expected some sort of geometrical device on the flagstone where the spot of light makes its appearance, but the stone slab is in fact quite bare except for a 7/8″ brass pin or 'clou' set back 6¼″ from one end. Whilst I was busy measuring the flagstone, a young fellow who had been sitting quietly on a bench with his girlfriend approached to discuss the 'phenomenon'. We were still about three hours in advance of noon, which is about 1350 hours local time at Chartres – he said it was better to be early on account of the crowds!

My new friend also explained how after the spot of light had crossed the flagstone, various coloured lights would appear on the floor in quick succession. He furnished me with a diagram and related how in 1975 a gentleman had carried out a fascinating experiment with the coloured, projected lights. He had placed on the flagstone three small emeralds. Subtly, the first emerald had changed into violet like amethyst, the third became alexandrite (indigo colour) and the second whitened slowly, becoming chalky and eventually changing into a diamond.

It seems that the sun crossing the flagstone acts as a herald for the real spectacle, which is a series of beautifully coloured lights or a succession of letters changing every few minutes.

Today we send radio signals into space, hoping to make contact with other intelligences. Some of these series of dots and dashes may be decoded to form the picture of a man. Likewise, one of the earlier spacecraft carried a plaque depicting a man and a woman along with a few binary numbers. Should it be so odd then, that someone should enshrine a message for us all those years ago? A message which may only be visible once a year but which, when decoded, may enable man to reach the stars.

On the day of my visit to Chartres, there was indeed a large crowd gathered around the flagstone. This is by complete contrast to many other churches, where not only are there no 'observers' but even the clergy seem totally unaware that anything out of the ordinary is about to happen. It seems that any secrets long entrusted to the church have been totally lost by the present day incumbents who often cover up old floors with carpets, rostrums etc and sometimes as at Orleans, officially close the church from 12-2pm so that one would have no opportunity to observe anything at all!

Unfortunately on my day at Chartres, the sky was slightly overcast. The circle of light made a few brief appearance as permitted between the clouds, and evoked a few gasps of admiration from the audience. After the signal event, the crowd quickly dispersed, unaware that the other phenomenon was about to begin.

Ely Cathedral 14ᵗʰ century pavement

In the hope that a similar event to the Chartres solstice might take place in an English cathedral, I became a frequent visitor to the cathedral at Ely, usually entering the west door a few minutes before noon.

The porch leads immediately into the labyrinth under the west tower and the longest nave in England, its floor decorated with a recurring motif of circles and squares set out in cubits of 25.25″, 30″ and 33″. The heart of the church is the magnificent octagonal lantern tower, 72ft in diameter, designed by the Sacrist Alan of Walsingham in 1322.

To the right of the octagon is the South Transept containing a remarkable pavement also dating to the 14th century. The pavement has almost been worn smooth with the years but one can still recognise the interesting cartwheel design.

The pavement at Ely

The centremost circle is a sacred decimal foot of 10″ and the wheel is just over 7ft in diameter, with a radius of 1,000mm to the ends of the 'spokes'.

In the window above the cartwheel pavement are to be seen two small holes about ½″ in diameter. When the sun shines strongly, about noon, these holes project brilliant pools of light onto the floor of the transept. These 'lunules' shimmer, hover and dance their way across the floor as the sun moves round and at the same time a host of other beautifully coloured lights are thrown onto the floors and walls of the cathedral.

Throughout the year, the two matched pools of light move from the south transept right across to the wall of the north transept opposite, and back again. At the time of the Spring Equinox, they have reached the pavement.

A few days later, they begin to approach the very centre of the 'cartwheel' Just before noon, the sign of the heart is flashed high up on a column next to the transept, then the pools of light begin to cross the pavement. At noon, the first pool of light settles exactly on the centre circle for a few brief moments before continuing its eternal journey. The event is repeated by the second lunule about three days later, suggesting that they may have been originally intended to mark the Easter events when Christ rose from the tomb after three days. Certain it is however, that at this time, the Earth on its elliptical orbit will have reached its mean distance from the sun.

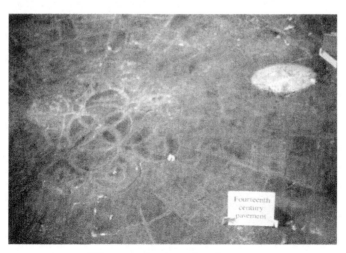

The sunspot approaches the centre.

Chapter 8

Atoms in Space

THE ATOM is named after the Greek word for indivisible and is the basic unit from which all substances are made. Its organisation is similar to the sun and revolving planets since in its simplest form it comprises a positively charged proton and an orbiting electron. The mass of the electron is almost negligible compared to that of the proton; it orbits the proton at a considerable distance and as the diameter of the proton is only about a 10,000th that of the orbit contained by the electron, the atom and all matter could be said to consist of empty space! The scale is such that if the Sun were considered to be a proton, then its orbiting electron would be found somewhere out beyond the furthest known planet, Pluto.

The chemical properties of the atom are fixed by the number of protons in the nucleus, which also gives the atom its atomic number. The number of protons is identical to the number of electrons since each positive proton has to have an orbiting electron. Should an atom give up or gain a proton, the element would be transformed into that of another substance. For each proton in the nucleus, there is usually, but not always, an accompanying neutral particle called the neutron. If the atom has a different number of neutrons to protons, it is known as an isotope. The number of protons plus neutron in the nucleus gives the atom its atomic mass number.

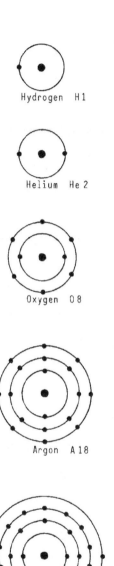

Hydrogen H 1

Helium He 2

Oxygen O 8

Argon A 18

Iron Fe 26

Hydrogen then, with one proton and one electron has the distinction of being the atomic No 1. When its nucleus comprises a proton plus a neutron, its mass is doubled and it is known as Heavy Hydrogen or Deuterium.

Atoms of a similar nature combine to form an element of a substance, but when different atoms combine, they form molecules of a compound. The electrons form a cloud as they spin around the nucleus. They are all identical with the same electrical charge but have to occupy fixed energy orbits or levels and these determine the nature of the substance and its willingness to combine with others. The electron cannot remain in a forbidden

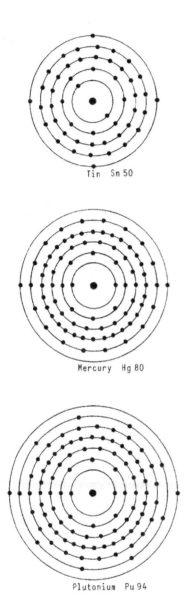

Tin Sn 50

Mercury Hg 80

Plutonium Pu 94

level although it may cross it to occupy a permitted band.

The Pythagorean maxim that "all things are numbers" is tailor made for the world of the atom. The energy levels consist of some seven 'shells' known as the k shell, l,m,n,o,p and q shells but in the more complex structures these shells divide again into sub-shells. The innermost shell can hold a maximum of two electrons. When it has only one electron i.e. Hydrogen, it is unstable and can react with other substances but when both electrons are present, ie. Helium, the shell is complete and the element stable. The next shell can hold eight electrons and the following shell 18 electrons so that the 'magic numbers' for the orbits are 2, 8, 18, 32, 50, 82 and 126.

Where the distribution of electrons in the outer shell displays a regular symmetry, the electrons are tightly bound together and the shell closed as if it had its full complement of electrons. Elements whose outer shells are closed are particularly stable such as Neon, Argon, Krypton, Xenon and Radon, all with eight electrons in the outer shell and together with Helium making up the inert gases. If the outer shell contains only one electron, or no electrons, the atom is chemically active as it seeks to stabilise its condition. An element such as Carbon, with four electrons out of a possible eight in the outer shell, will readily share this shell with another element, thus combining to form a new compound.

The number of protons in the atom allows a table to be drawn up – the atomic number – which allows one to predict the behaviour of a particular element. Over 100 elements are known but where the number of protons exceeds 90, the atom will actively throw out particles in an attempt to stabilise its form through a transmutation known as spontaneous decay.

The Uranium atom has 92 electrons, dispersed as follows from the innermost shell outwards; 2, 8, 18, 12, and 2 electrons; its naturally occurring form is the isotope U238 with a mass of 238 (the sum of protons plus neutrons). it is the heaviest naturally occurring element with 92 protons and actively emits radiation and surplus neutrons in an attempt to stabilise its condition. Heavier elements may have existed but by now would have completely decayed, although they can be manufactured artificially such as Plutonium with 94 protons.

When the atom seeks to change its form in this way, it ejects neutrons along with alpha, beta and gamma radiation and of course, energy. A neutron thus ejected may enter another nucleus if its kinetic energy is compatible but in so doing it disrupts this nucleus so that it splits up and also throws out neutrons and radiation. The reaction is virtually instantaneous and known as fission. The process may continue and be self-sustaining if a certain minimum quantity of material is available. This quantity is called the critical mass and the bringing together of two or more sub-critical masses produced the phenomenon of the chain reaction with its massive release of energy commonly known as The Bomb.

In the nuclear reactor, the reaction is controlled by alternating the fuel rods with rods of an element such as Boron or Hafnium, which will readily absorb the excess emitted neutrons. The control rods are raised until the reaction starts and the reaction can be governed by further raising or lowering of the control rods. When the fuel begins to become exhausted, the fission products also absorb neutrons so a secondary set of rods is provided and can be progressively withdrawn to compensate for this. A third set of rods called Scram Rods can be injected into the core at any time to shut down the plant in the event of an emergency.

Many of the emitted neutrons are wasted as instead of causing fission, they may be absorbed by other materials present or the boundary walls of the reactor. They can be deflected back to the core by surrounding the core with a suitable screen such as graphite. The critical mass in the reactor is influenced by the type of fuel and geometry of the fuel and moderator (if used) elements.

The approaching neutron must have a kinetic energy similar to that of the nucleus it seeks to enter in order to be absorbed. Before it can cause fission of the Uranium isotope U235, it has to be slowed down and this is done with the help of a moderator. The moderator should ideally have a mass similar to that of the neutron and Deuterium, (with a single neutron and proton)in the form of heavy hydrogen in 'heavy' water is convenient since it can be circulated around the rods as a coolant.

If ordinary or 'light' water were to be used, the mass of the fuel elements would need to be greater. The coolant is pumped around the fuel rods and then to the heat exchanger to generate steam. Carbon in the form of graphite rods is also a suitable moderator and used in British reactors but substances heavier than carbon have too great a mass to be employed.

Theoretically the fuel may be solid, liquid or a gas, but solid fuel is generally used, the fuel elements being enclosed in a thin skin of stainless steel to facilitate handling and avoid contamination of the coolant. The moderator, if required, may be graphite, heavy or light water or beryllium and the coolant heavy or light water, a gas or liquid metal; Winscale has an advanced gas cooled reactor, the coolant reaching 1000°F at the outlet.

simple cubic cell

additional atom in centre

extra atom in face centre

simple cubic cell

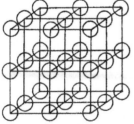

The cells are like
building blocks
which fit together
to form the structure
of the crystal

Reactors in which the neutron is slowed down with a moderator are known as 'slow' or thermal reactors and those which employ the uranium isotope U238, as 'fast' reactors.

The fuel may be an isotope of uranium or the artificially produced plutonium. By arranging a blanket of natural uranium around the reactor core, the blanket is bombarded with neutrons and converted into plutonium. This type of reactor is known as a 'breeder' reactor such as the Dounreay fast breeder which produces more fuel than it consumes.

The core has to be shielded from the environment and a casing of suitable material such as earth, water, concrete or steel can be used. The casing is often spherical to give maximum resistance to the internal coolant

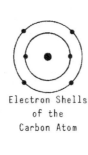

Electron Shells
of the
Carbon Atom

Diamond

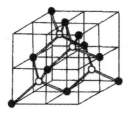

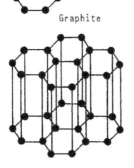

Graphite

pressure and may contain neutron absorbing materials within concentric layers of stainless steel.

The Dounreay reactor produces power as well as fuel, and isotopes for scientific applications may be created in the blanket as a continuing programme of research is essential for this developing industry.

Fusion is the name given to another nuclear process where a new atom is created and a massive amount of energy released. The prime example is the Sun, which is a continuous thermo nuclear reaction, the process was identified and named the Carbon Cycle by two German physicists in 1939. Carbon begins the cycle and four protons are converted into energy of the order of about 25 million electron volts

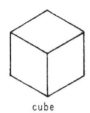

cube

cube

interpenetrating
cubes

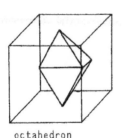

octahedron

thus creating an atom of Helium.

Atoms are the smallest units from which all elements and compounds are made. The structure of virtually all solids is crystalline, i.e. they follow a repetitive geometrical pattern and we might say that a crystal is a three dimensional arrangement of points in space. Glass is a curious exception, in that although apparently a solid, it is actually a super-cooled liquid with the internal structure of a liquid.

With a pure element all the atoms are identical and the mixing of types of atoms results in a new substance – the compound. With most metals the atoms are closely packed together and if we think of them as a layer of say, tennis balls, which we pack together on the floor of a box, then we have the choice with a second layer either to fit them onto the spaces between the balls of the first layer, or to arrange them directly above the balls of the first layer.

With most metals the atoms behave just like spheres and adopt either of these arrangements, being 'close packed' with either a hexagonal or cubic structure. The cube may be described as either face-centred or body-centred according to the arrangement of the atoms. Copper, silver, gold and gamma iron (y fe) are all face-centred cubic structures with co-ordinate numbers of 12.

The crystals of copper and diamond (carbon) are octahedral which belongs to the cubic system and silver, germanium and grey tin all follow the diamond structure.

All elements can be regarded as either metals or non-metals. Metals are dense and conduct electricity while non-metals are poor conductors and can be used as insulators.

Carbon is unusual in that it displays the properties of a metal and non-metal so that it can be described as metalloid. It has a high melting point and is not very dense yet conducts electricity. It crystallises in two forms, as diamond and graphite, which are almost totally opposite in character. Diamond crystallises octahedrally within the cubic structure and may be described as one atom surrounded tetrahedrally by four others. The structure consists of four such units giving the impression of the face-centred cube and because of the disposition of the individual atoms, it is the hardest substance known to man.

By contrast, graphite is soft and flakey and belongs to the hexagonal structure. The layers of atoms slide easily over one another making graphite a good lubricant.

Carbon atoms have a valency of four, so have four 'vacancies' on the outer electron shell. This enables them to combine easily with other substances and accounts for the prolific variety of carbon based substances including man himself.

Silicon is an element similar to carbon in that it will combine readily with other substances, with metals to form silicates and with hydro-carbons to form silicones, which make good electrical insulators.

Copper is an excellent conductor of electricity and has been widely used in the manufacture of power cables, but due to its relatively highcost, like gold and silver it has almost become a 'precious' metal and has been replaced by aluminium.

Aluminium is, perhaps surprisingly, the most plentiful metal after iron, but extraction from its ore, bauxite, requires large quantities of electricity which makes it an expensive metal. Being of light weight, it is extremely useful in the aircraft industry and can be alloyed with other metals for greater strength and wider applications.

The densest and most valuable metals are silver, gold and platinum. Lead is also one of the densest metals but being relatively plentiful renders it valueless as a base for a monetary system. Gold can be drawn into extremely fine wire or beaten into wafer thin, almost transparent sheets and since it does not readily combine with oxygen, like lead or iron to form 'rust', but is more often melted down into bullion to disappear into the bank vaults of the world's treasuries.

It may be difficult at first to identify to which crystal system a crystal may belong. There are many hundreds of types of crystal and they can all be reconciled to seven basic classes although exactly which class may not at first sight be apparent.

If we take a cube for example, we could slice pieces off the corners or edges to give the crystal a more rounded appearance, or completely remove the edges to leave an octahedron; so the octahedron is finally envisaged as suspended in a cube.

When the Alchemists melted lead or silver in a pot, they were temporarily breaking down the crystalline structure of the metal. When a metal is heated to become a liquid, the atoms leave the regular arrangement and jump around at random. The substance can be poured because the atoms have no geometrical bond to each other. By introducing the "grain of the stone", the alchemist seems to have been seeding his brew to change it to another metal.

Seeding is the normal procedure for growing crystals. In commercial crystal growing, the metal is introduced to the seed in a high pressure vacuum. A typical method uses the Crochralski crystal pulling' technique. The melt is maintained in the vacuum chamber just above melting point and heat is abstracted through the seed crystal, which 'grows' in consequence. The new crystal grows onto the seed and may reach a length of 5 or 7", germanium crystals can attain a weight of over 5kg using this method.

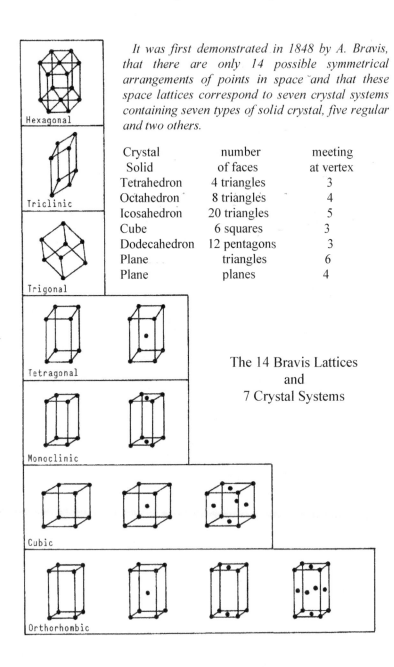

Hexagonal

Triclinic

Trigonal

Tetragonal

Monoclinic

Cubic

Orthorhombic

It was first demonstrated in 1848 by A. Bravis, that there are only 14 possible symmetrical arrangements of points in space and that these space lattices correspond to seven crystal systems containing seven types of solid crystal, five regular and two others.

Crystal Solid	number of faces	meeting at vertex
Tetrahedron	4 triangles	3
Octahedron	8 triangles	4
Icosahedron	20 triangles	5
Cube	6 squares	3
Dodecahedron	12 pentagons	3
Plane	triangles	6
Plane	planes	4

The 14 Bravis Lattices
and
7 Crystal Systems

Silicone crystals are also grown using this technique. The large crystal is then finely sliced to produce many small 'chips', each a miniature of the parent and with identical characteristics. The crystal or chip may be used as a rectifier to modify the direction of an electric current and can thus convey or store information.

To grow a diamond, pressures of around 20-100,000 bars and temperatures of 3,500K are required. This has been achieved by the GEC of America in a specially devised apparatus and the subsequent diamonds are used industrially such as in hard wearing tips for drills.

The most recent and futuristic application of the crystal is in the development of the Laser – "Light Amplification by the Stimulated Emission of Radiation". Light is bounced within the crystal until it emerges as a high intensity beam of light of radio frequency. it has many potential uses in the fields of space and atomic research as well as in medicine and telecommunications.

Chapter 9

Decoding Ezekiel's Temple

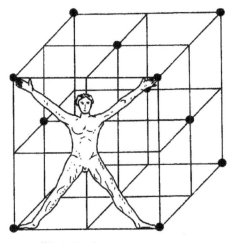

"Behold, there was a man....
...and he stood in the gate."

Ezekiel's Description of the Holy City

Ezekiel 40

"In the five and twentieth year of our captivity, in the beginning of the year, in the tenth day of the month, in the fourteenth year after that the city was smitten, in the selfsame day the hand of the lord was upon me, and brought me thither.

In the visions of God brought he me into the land of Israel, and set me upon a very high mountain, by which was as the frame of a city on the south.

And he brought me thither, and, behold, there was a man, whose appearance was like the appearance of brass, with a line of flax in his hand, and a measuring reed; and he stood in the gate.

And the man said unto me, Son of man, behold with thine eyes, and hear with thine ears, and set thine heart upon all that I shall show thee; for to the intent that I might shew them unto thee art thou brought hither: declare all that thou seest to the house of Israel.

And behold a wall on the outside of the house round about, and in the man's hand a measuring reed of six cubits long by the cubit and an hand breadth: so he measured the breadth of the building, one reed: and the height, one reed.

The came he unto the gate which looketh toward the east, and went up the stairs thereof, and measured the threshold of the gate, which was one reed broad; and the other threshold of the gate, which was one reed broad.

And every little chamber was one reed long, and one reed broad; and between the little chambers were five cubits; and the threshold of the gate by the porch of the gate within was one reed.

He measured also the porch of the gate within, one reed.

The measured he the porch of the gate, eight cubits; and the posts thereof, two cubits; and the porch of the gate was inward.

And the little chambers of the gate eastward were three on this side, and three on that side; they three were of one measure: and the posts had one measure on this side and on that.

And he measured the breadth of the entry of the gate, ten cubits; and the length of the gate, thirteen cubits.

The space also before the little chambers was one cubit on this side, and the space was one cubit on that side: and the little chambers were six cubits on this side, and six cubits on that side.

He measured then the gate from the roof of one little chamber to the roof of another: the breadth was five and twenty cubits, door against door.

He made also posts of threescore cubits, even unto the post of the court round about the gate.

And from the face of the gate of the entrance unto the face of the porch of the inner gate were fifty cubits.

And there were narrow windows to the little chambers, and to their posts within the gate round about, and likewise to the arches: and windows were round about inward: and upon each post were palm trees.

Then brought he me into the outward court, and, lo, there were chambers, and a pavement made for the court round about: thirty chambers were upon the pavement.

And the pavement by the side of the gates over against the length of the gates was the power pavement.

Then he measured the breadth from the forefront on the lower gate unto the forefront of the inner court without, an hundred cubits eastward and northward.

And the gate of the outward court that looked toward the north, he measured the length thereof, and the breadth thereof.

And the little chambers thereof were three on this side and three on that side; and the posts thereof and the arches thereof were after the measure of the first gate: the length thereof was fifty cubits, and the breadth five and twenty cubits.

And their windows, and their arches, and their palm trees, were after the measure of the gate that looketh toward the east; and they went up unto it by seven steps; and the arches thereof were before them.

And the gate of the inner court was over against the gate toward the north, and toward the east; and he measured from gate to gate an hundred cubits.

And after that he brought me toward the south, and behold a gate toward the south: and he measured the posts thereof and the arches thereof according to these measures.

And there were windows in it and in the arches thereof round about, like those windows: the length was fifty cubits, and the breadth five and twenty cubits.

And there were seven steps to go up to it, and the arches thereof were before them: and it had palm trees, one on this side, and another on that side, upon the posts thereof.

And there was a gate in the inner court toward the south: and he measured from gate to gate toward the south an hundred cubits.

And he brought me to the inner court by the south gate: and he measured the gate according to these measures.

And the little chambers thereof, and the posts thereof, and the arches thereof, according to these measures: and there were windows in it and in the arches thereof round about: it was fifty cubits long, and five and twenty cubits broad.

And the arches round about were five and twenty cubits long, and five cubits broad.

And the arches thereof were toward the utter court; and palm trees were upon the posts thereof; and the going up to it had eight steps.

And he brought me into the inner court toward the east: and he measured the gate according to these measures.

And the little chambers thereof, and the posts thereof, and the arches thereof, were according to these measures: and there were windows therein and in the arches thereof round about: it was fifty cubits long, and five and twenty cubits broad.

And the arches thereof were toward the outward court; and palm trees were upon the posts thereof, on this side, and on that side: and the going up to it had eight steps.

And he brought me to the north gate, and measured it according to these measures;

The little chambers thereof, the posts thereof, and the arches thereof, and the windows to it round about: the length was fifty cubits, and the breadth five and twenty cubits.

And the posts thereof were toward the utter court; and palm trees were upon the posts thereof, on this side, and on that side: and the going up to it had eight steps."

Ezekiel 41

"Afterward he brought me to the temple, and measured the posts, six cubits broad on the one side, and six cubits broad on the other side, which was the breadth of the tabernacle.

And the breadth of the door was ten cubits; and the sides of the door were five cubits on the one side, and five cubits on the other side: and he measured the length thereof, forty cubits: and the breadth, twenty cubits.

So he measured the length thereof, twenty cubits; and the breadth, twenty cubits, before the temple: and he said unto me, This is the most holy place.

After he measured the wall of the house, six cubits; and the breadth of every side chamber, four cubits, round about the house on every side.

And the side chambers were three, one over another, and thirty in order; and they entered into the wall which was of the house for the side chambers round about, that they might have hold, but they had not hold in the wall of the house.

And there was an enlarging, and a winding about still upward to the side chambers: for the winding about of the house went still upward round about the house: therefore the breadth of the house was still upward, and so increased from the lowest chamber to the highest by the midst.

I saw also the height of the house round about: the foundations of the side chambers were a full reed of six great cubits.

The thickness of the wall, which was for the side chambers without, was five cubits: and that which was left was the place of the side chambers that were within.

And between the chambers was the wideness of twenty cubits round about the house on every side.

And the doors of the side chambers were toward the place that was left, one door toward the north, and another door toward the south: and the breadth of the place that was left was five cubits round about."

Ezekiel 42

"Then he brought me forth into the utter court, the way toward the north: and he brought me into the chamber that was over against the separate place, and which was before the building toward the north.

Before the length of an hundred cubits was the north door, and the breadth was fifty cubits.

Over against the twenty cubits which were for the inner court, and over against the pavement which was for the utter court, was gallery against gallery in three stories.

And before the chambers was a walk of ten cubits breadth inward, a way of one cubit; and their doors toward the north.

Now the upper chambers were shorter: for the galleries were higher than these, than the lower, and than the middlemost of the building.

For they were in three stories, but had not pillars as the pillars of the courts: therefore the building was straightened more than the lowest and the middlemost from the ground.

And the wall that was without over against the chambers, toward the utter court on the forepart of the chambers, the length thereof was fifty cubits.

For the length of the chambers that were in the utter court was fifty cubits: and. lo, before the temple were an hundred cubits.

And from under these chambers was the entry on the east side, as one goeth into them from the utter court.

The chambers were in the thickness of the wall of the court toward the east, over against the separate place, and over against the building.

And the way before them was like the appearance of the chambers which were toward the north, as long as they, and as broad as they: and all their goings out were both according to their fashions, and according to their doors.

Now when he had made an end of measuring the inner house, he brought me forth toward the gate whose prospect is toward the east, and measured it round about.

He measured the east side with the measuring reed, five hundred reeds, with the measuring reed round about.

He measured the north side, five hundred reeds, with the measuring reed round about.

He measured the south side, five hundred reeds, with the measuring reed.

He turned about to the west side, and measured five hundred reeds with the measuring reed.

He measured it by the four sides: it had a wall round about, five hundred reeds long, and five hundred broad, to make a separation between the sanctuary and the profane place."

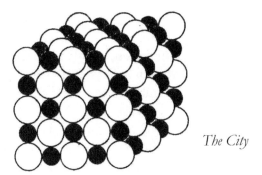

The City

Reading through Ezekiel's description of the Holy City, it is easy to get lost in the labyrinth of measurements, courtyards and chambers. We are lucky indeed if we can read beyond the first paragraph at all, because on first reading, the description would appear to be nonsense. The breadth of the building, height of the building, threshold of the gate, breadth of the chambers and porch of the gate within are all one reed.

Yet Ezekiel went to extreme lengths to record all the measurements of the city, so was his 'vision' some nonsensical hallucination, or a technical description of something beyond his knowledge and possibly beyond ours? If one knew what he was trying to describe, it could be that in fact, he has left us a brilliant description which has lain dormant for thousands of years until the time when a civilisation should be sufficiently advanced scientifically to comprehend it.

"Behold, there was a man, whose appearance was like the appearance of brass, with a line of flax in his hand, and a measuring reed; and he stood in the gate."

"And in the man's hand a measuring reed of six great cubits long by the cubit and an hand breadth." Here again is a curiosity, was the reed shaped like a plank? - six cubits long and a cubit and a hand broad. Was the cubit and an hand meant to denote the circumference or diameter of the pole or reed?

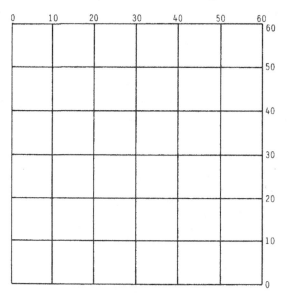

A Lattice Array of 60 x 60 cubits.

He is indicating here that the cubit in use is no ordinary cubit, but a special cubit, the length of a normal cubit plus a hand. It is usually considered that the reed was a pole consisting of six such cubits in length.

Let us consider the repetition of identical measurements; this could easily be taken as an indication of a crystal structure, and indeed, the dimensions of the city can only be decoded if we begin by considering the city as a crystal. The

The Unit Cell of 10 x 10 cubits

chamber is one reed and the city is one reed. A reed is six cubits and the city is six cubits ... or 60 cubits or 600 cubits or 6,000 cubits. Once we have identified the basic 'unit cell', the same structure will be repeated everywhere.

On a lattice of 10 x 10 cubits, we arrange a basic unit cell, one chamber of 6 cubits on each corner and one in the centre. This leaves a space, horizontally and vertically between the chambers, of 4 cubits. This space could also be described as a hole, cell or chamber. In this case a chamber of 4 cubits, found later in Ezekiel's description as the "side chambers of 4 cubits round about the house on every side."

The side chambers have no hold in the wall of the house since they are not of the primary structure. "They entered into the wall of the house for the side chambers round about, that they might have hold, but they had not hold in the wall of the house."

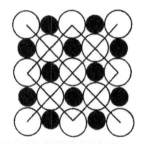

The entire structure can be filled with chambers of 6 cubits, side chambers of 4 cubits, and diagonal spaces of 1 cubit. We must remember though, that our crystal is three-dimensional and it is necessary to consider the next 'layer' above. Our lattice array is 10 cubits square yet "between the little chambers were 5 cubits." Now if we take our second layer of chambers and place it on top of the first layer, the chambers of 6 cubits would settle on top of the chambers of 4 cubits so that if we look down vertically, we would see a lattice array of 5 cubits.

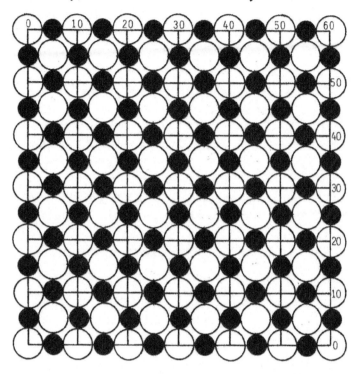

The Structure

Suppose we now shrink ourselves down into the array, take a walk amongst the chambers and see what measurements we can find.

We can see from the figure that the diagonal space between the chambers is 1 cubit. "The space also before the little chambers was one cubit on this side, and one cubit on that side: and the little chambers were six cubits on this side, and six cubits on that side."

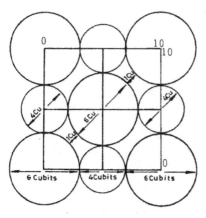

The Unit Cell

By pairing off two chambers, or two chambers on this side and two chambers on that side, we begin to create the gates and porches.

The length of the gate is 13 cubits (2 chambers of 6 cubits plus a space of 1 cubit); the porch of the gate is 8 cubits (1 chamber of 6 and 2 spaces or "posts" of 1 cubit).

Not only do we have to try and fit the pieces of

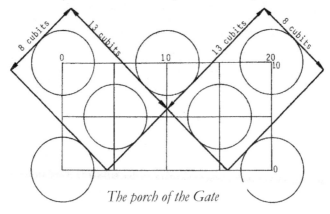

The porch of the Gate

this space-age jig-saw puzzle together, but we have to look into the dimensions provided to construct the pieces.

One of the fundamental units of the city is the "court of the gate".

"He made posts of sixty cubits even unto the post of the gate." Our gate of 13 x 8 cubits fits our array of 60 cubits in such a way, that by locking gates ands porches in around the perimeter, we are left with a central 'courtyard'.

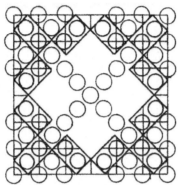

The Court of the Gate

Entering from the lower left-hand gate, there are now seven 'steps' up to the opposite gate, and the distance is 50 cubits (7 chambers of 6 cubits and 8 spaces of 1 cubit). That would fit in well with Ezekiel's description "from the face of the gate of the entrance unto the face of the porch of the inner gate were 50 cubits."

We now encounter an irreconcilable difficulty in that "he measured then the gate from the roof of one little chamber to the roof of another: the breadth was five and twenty cubits, door against door."

The outer gates are identical. The term "gate" is used somewhat loosely as is "court" when describing features of the city.

"The posts thereof and the arches thereof were after the measure of the first gate the length thereof was fifty cubits, and the breadth five and twenty cubits.".…. "the arches round about were five and twenty cubits long, and five cubits broad." Our problem here is that no matter where we look on our arrays based n multiples or courts of 60 x 60 cubits, we cannot find gates of 50 x 25 cubits.

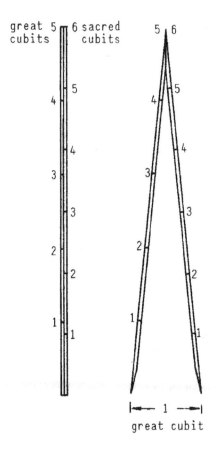

great 5 ╓ 6 sacred
cubits ║ cubits

|←— 1 —→|
great cubit

The key to the translation of the cubits lies in an analysis of the Reed. here is the Golden Reed referred to in the Revelation of St. John. We now have to reconsider our reed that measures six cubits by the cubit and an hand. Ezekiel states that "the foundations of the side chambers were a full reed of six great cubits." This implies that there may have been a lesser reed in use whose value was less than six great cubits, also that there may have been a cubit whose value was normal, the addition of the extra hand making it a 'great' cubit.

Now if the normal cubit were the sacred cubit of 25 inches, then given a hand of 5 inches, the great cubit would be 30 inches in length. 5 hands make a sacred cubit and 6 hands make a great cubit; 5 great cubits make a sacred reed and 6 great cubits make a full great reed of 15ft.

When the angel is at an end of measuring the city, he finally measures the gate whose prospect is towards the east. He measures the east, north, south, and west sides, each 500 reeds with the measuring reed round about. Why did he not use the line of flax for such a long distance? If his measuring reed were nothing but a simple pole, what a tedious business it would be, laying the pole down on the ground, marking the end and stepping it along 500 times for the final measurement.

If instead of a simple pole, our reed were a giant pair of dividers, hinged at the top and opening out to

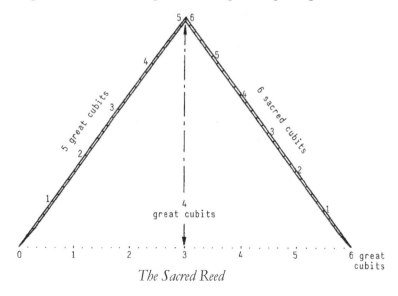

The Sacred Reed

1 great cubit, how much simpler it would be to measure the city. But if instead of opening out to 1 great cubit, our reed opened out to measure a full great reed of 6 great cubits, then stepping out 500 reeds would be simplicity itself and what a beautiful instrument we would have.

One arm of the reed is graduated into 6 sacred cubits and the other arm into 5 great cubits.

When fully open, the height of the instrument is 4 great cubits, half the base is 3 great cubits and together with the arm of 5 great cubits we are presented with two Pythagorean 3-4-5 triangles, the same triangles with which, according to Plato, the structure of the Cosmos was built.

King James gathered together the finest scholars in the land to prepare his authorised version of the bible. it is clear that Ezekiel was talking about chambers with entries, yet a very popular modern translation considers this to be guardhouses with sentries! By converting cubits into metres, the whole meaning would be rendered allegorical and useless. Not for nothing was King James held to be "the wisest fool in Christendom". He ruled by "divine right" and "dieu et mon droit" is still the family motto today. But neither the modern nor original translators seem to have realised that there were two values of cubit.

Looking back now to our court of 60 x 60 cubits, it is easy to find the gate of 50 x 25 cubits. We have been working so far in sacred cubits. 60 sacred cubits = 50 great cubits and 30 sacred cubits = 25 great cubits. The arches of 5 cubits breadth are formed by cutting through the chambers of 6 sacred cubits (6 sacred cubits = 5 great cubits).

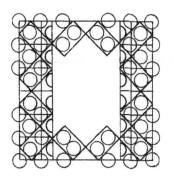

The Gate
50 x 25 cubits

Here then, is the second unit of the crystal city.

After describing the gate, or gates, the angel "brought he me into the outer court, and lo, there were chambers, and a pavement made for the court round about; thirty chambers were upon the pavement."

The pavement is constructed by overlapping diagonally, two of our basic 60 x 60 court units. It is a fundamental unit of the city and enables Ezekiel and his guide to walk down the

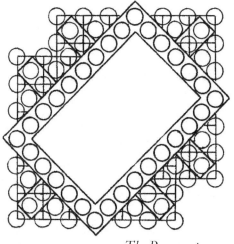

The Pavement

pavement and enter another, larger, court.

"Then he measured the breadth from the forefront of the lower gate unto the forefront of the inner court without, an hundred cubits eastward and northward." This court of 100 cubits is simply an open space, an absence of lesser courts or pavements. It is part of the array structure as 100 great cubits equal 120 sacred cubits.

The court of 100 cubits is also a fundamental unit since it is repeated throughout the structure. It is also the unit of the inner temple or house. "So he

The Inner Temple

measured the house, an hundred cubits long."

We can now re-arrange the innermost court thus formed according to the dimensions of the inner temple…..

These then, are the pieces which go to make up the crystalline city.

St John describes the city as lying foursquare, *"the length and the breadth and the height of it are equal."*

The city is seen as a cube.

For St John, the angel measured the city twice, first according to Divine measure, when it measured 12,000 "furlongs", or more correctly, great cubits, and second when he "measured the wall thereof, an hundred and forty and four cubits, *according to the measure of a man*, that is, of the angel."

$$12,000 \text{ great cubits} = 360,000'' = 14400 \text{ sacred cubits}$$

This is the perimeter of the wall and the "measure of a man" is therefore the sacred cubit, given him by the Lord through the angel.

Each base side measures 3,000 great cubits which is the 500 great reeds of Ezekiel (6 great cubits to the great reed). Ezekiel goes on to tell us "the wall of the city had twelve foundations." Each "foundation" is an edge of the cube and the edges have a total length of 36,000 great cubits.

Each base side of 3,000 great cubits is 3,600 sacred cubits and into each side we could insert 60 of our courts of 60 sacred cubits. The total number of courts at base level would be 60 times 60 or 3600 which is the square of 60 and the total for the whole configuration would be – the cube of 60.

When the knights returned from the Crusades, they constructed the Church of St. Sepulchre or 'Round Church' in Cambridge. Built in 1130, it stands opposite St. John's College which falls in its parish and itself occupies the site of St. John's Hospital. The design of the church is based on that of the Dome of the Rock and the church of St. Sepulchre in Jerusalem containing the tomb of Our Lord.

The centre of the church takes the form of a sunken, tiled well. Each tile is 6″ square and may be

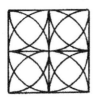

A block of four tiles from the Round Church

likened to the chambers of Ezekiel's city which were each 6 cubits. A single tile has the design of a double lenticle and four tiles join together to make a circle within a square – or a sphere within a cube.

The well is 210″ or 10 grail cubits in diameter and is given a pattern through the tiles which either include or exclude the geometric device. A raised stone collar 54″ wide surrounds the well and on it stand the eight massive Norman pillars supporting the roof.

Each pillar is 21″ or 1 grail cubit in radius and the radius of the base is 25″ or 1 sacred cubit; since there are eight pillars, the collar can be seen to support an octagonal symmetry.

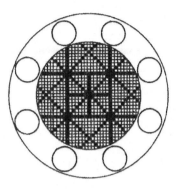

The Octagon, the Hexagon, and the Cube, these are all powerful Christian motifs.

The crystal nature of the city has already been indicated, but whether it was actually a crystal or something akin to it is still an open question.

If it were simply a crystal then enough clues are presented to identify what it

Interior of the Round Church

was a crystal of.   If you were God, which crystal or structure would you choose? The molecule of the Grail ratio, Hydrogen 2, Oxygen 1 = water. Salt? an essential substance which man cannot do without? Carbon? the most essential element for all forms of life? Carbon has two crystal forms. As diamond, it is the hardest substance known to man and crystallises octahedrally within the cubic system. As graphite, it follows the hexagonal structure and can be used as a moderator in the geometrically arranged core of a nuclear reactor. Carbon is the only atom to comprise six electrons and six protons. You might call it the only atom to have twelve 'apostles'. Was this the holiest of holiest in the temple?

The hexagonal core
of the Dounreay reactor

Photo by courtesy of UKAE

The Golden Reed

HERSCHEL and Newton divided the polar radius of the Earth into ten million (10,000,000) sacred cubits of 25" as the most scientific unit of measure for this planet. This would have given a diameter of 500,000,000 sacred inches. It might have been more proper to divide the polar diameter into 1 (1,000,000,000) units which are basic units which would be half-inches and which we could perhaps call diametric units or diametrons making the inch a double unit. This is more like a 'sacred' division since it comprises 10 digits and represents the totality of the decimal system in as much as you count up to nine then start again.

The diameter divided decimally into 10 or multiples of 10 automatically gives a circumference equal to the pi (Π) figure since the circumference is calculated as pi x diameter.

The diameter of 1,000,000,000 basic units or diametrons (half-inches) comprises 10,000 sacred miles of 10,000 sacred hands of 10 diametrons and gives a circumference for the perfect sphere equal to pi, i.e. 3145926530 diametrons or half-inches.

The decimal division of the polar axis corresponds to the sexagesimal division of the circumference of the sphere. The circumference is usually divided into 360 degrees of 60 miles of 6,000ft of 12 inches

The beauty of this method of dividing the diameter decimally and the circumference sexagesimally is that the 'sacred' inch derived from

177

the diameter is for all practical purposes identical to the 'great' inch derived from the circumference. The actual polar circumference of the Earth, measured in English half-inches is 3144940000 and stands at 0.001 to the true figure for pi. But more interestingly, if we use a pure sphere of 360° x 60 nautical miles of 6000ft of 12 inches of 2 basic units and divide by 24 hours of 60 minute of 60 seconds and then divide by 36,000 we get exactly the same basic unit which we called a diametron of 1 (half-inch!).

It is interesting to note that the physical length of the old British half-penny was one inch. With the decimal currency, the same size mould or stamp was used to cast the new 2p coin; its length is therefore 2 diametrons!

Units derived from the diameter then, are 'sacred' units and those from the circumference, 'great' units; the great cubit therefore relates to the circumference as the sacred cubit relates to the diameter of a circle.

Archimedes, in his estimate of the circumference of the world gives a figure of 300,000 stadia. It is not generally realised that this figure is perfectly correct, since the Stadium here is not the geographic stadium (which would require 216,000 stadia but a "sacred" stadium of 500 sacred feet of 10".

This can be more positively clarified by the statement of Posidonius who gave a diameter to the Earth of 100,000 stadia and a circumference of 300,000 stadia. This was supposedly derived from stellar observations made at Thrace in Greece and Scyene in Egypt, the difference in declination of fixed stars being 24° and the linear distance 20,000 stadia. The answer seems to have been arrived at in a roundabout way since the actual distance from Thrace to Scyene is closer to 16° or 10,000 stadia. It would seem that a 'half' stadium of 300ft was used in conjunction with the stated 24° so that the true source of this estimate is uncertain.

The figure of 300,000 stades for the circumference is of course a rounded-off figure, like the molten sea in the Temple of Solomon, which had a diameter of 10 cubits and was encompassed by a line of 30 cubits.

Now one of the failings of the metre as a unit of measurement is that it is entirely decimal and does not readily lend itself to being divided into fractions. Accordingly, some legal people, who are given the problem of dividing up parcels of land, adopt a 'duodecimal' system using the metre and the old 'base 12' subdivisions.

What is required is a system incorporating both multiples of 10 and multiples of 12.

The first multiples of the basic diametric unit are the sacred hand of 10 diametrons (5") and the great hand of 12 diametrons (6"). Similarly, we have a sacred, decimal foot of 10" and a great foot of 12", both being two hands respectively.

The great cubit of 30" is the lowest common denominator between sacred hands and great hands since it has 6 hands of 10 diametrons (5") and 5 hands of 12 diametrons (6"). Again, the sacred reed is the lowest common denominator with 6 sacred cubits and 5 great cubits. It "honours the odd and the even" just as did the kings in Plato's Atlantis, who assembled every 5th or 6th year. One arm of the reed is divided decimally and the other duodecimally. One can thus choose between units of 10 or 12 as required, just as today we use rulers with millimetres on the one side and feet & inches on the other. When an extra great cubit is added to the reed, it become a full great reed of six great cubits (360 diametrons) and this is the instrument St. John describes as the Golden Reed. It was a "golden" reed quite simply because it was probably made of a metal such as a golden alloy, which would provide a durable surface on which to engrave the standard units of measurement.

For measuring short distances then, we might use the reed closed when we would take a figure from one of the arms or use the length of the staff as a gauge. For long distances, we would open the reed out and use it as a pace stick much in the fashion of an R.S.M. pacing out the steps of his soldiers.

the man-sized stick

The sacred reed, as already described is five cubits in length, an instrument of the Angel, but not of man.

A more man-sized 'dividers' would have a length of 30" – one great cubit. It would be divided into 6 hands of 10 diametrons on the one side and 5 hands of 12 diametrons on the other.

As a measuring stick, the arms swing out to give a full extent of 12 sacred hands and 10 great hands.

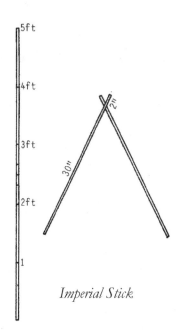

Imperial Stick

As a pacestick, it would have a maximum span of 36" – which is one English yard – a true yard stick!

Measuring a pace when fully open would give a pace of 6ft and 1,000 paces the geographic mile of 6,000ft. Setting the pace to 2 great cubits gives a mile of 5,000ft and setting to 2 sacred cubits the sacred mile of 5,000 decimal feet.

The illustration shows actual Imperial measuring stick. Each arm measures 30" up to the pivot and 2" beyond the pivot. The 2" extending beyond the pivot is necessary to give the stick support when it is extended to its full length of 60" or 5ft.

Professor Thom suggests that the megalithic yard was carried around as a stick having a length of 32.64"; if this is so, then it was only slightly longer than the stick described here.

As a pace-stick, a length of 32" would be marginally short of comfortable for a 6ft man to hold. If the length of the stick were increased by 0.64", the stick would have a length of 32.64" and be the ancient British megalithic yard. If the overall length of the stick were increased to 33", it would fit the man's hand perfectly and be the classical Sumerian or Babylonian yard of 50 shusi.

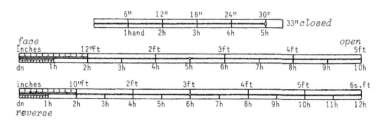

The Measuring Stick

The true measure of the man-sized stick then is the great cubit of 30" and the overall length the Sumerian yard of 33.0".

This yard of 33.0" has been found in the Indus Valley in Northern India where it was known as a gaz. It was divided into 25 'Indus Inches' or 50 Sumerian shusi so these two civilisations must at one time have had some common factor or communication. By logical extension, there must also have been a 'double yard' of 100 shusi, i.e. 66" which was the amount rolled out by the 21" diameter wheel. 12 revolutions gave the chain of 66ft so that the 'English' surveying chain actually comprises 1200 shusi or

> 12 double yards of 100 shusi
> 24 yards of 50 shusi
> 40 cubits of 30 shusi
> 60 feet of 20 shusi

100 links of 12 shusi
120 hands of 10 shusi

The Sumerian foot of 20 shusi later came to be called a 'Saxon' foot (13.2") and 10 cubits or 15 Saxon feet made the English pole (16.5 English feet) which was a quarter the length of the chain. The English furlong of 660ft is more correctly seen as 600 Sumerian feet or 400 Sumerian cubits.

Perhaps after all Geoffrey of Monmouth in his "History of the Kings of Britain" was not totally unjustified in making Brutus the first king of England.....

"Brutus, beyond the setting of the sun, past the realms of Gaul, there lies an island in the sea, once occupied by giants. Now it is empty and ready for your folk. Down the years this will prove an abode suited to you and your people, and for your descendants it will be a second Troy. A race of kings will be born there from your stock and the round circle of the whole earth will be subject to them."

Two acquaintances without military experience were asked to take ten normal steps. Each step when measured turned out to be 36".... 1,000 paces would have given the geographic mile of 6,000ft. Two acquaintances with military experience were asked to repeat the same experiment. Their steps proved to be 30" – giving the mile of the Legions – 5,000ft.

The Romans were great organisers of the military: they went everywhere in their hundreds (centurions) and their thousands. Marching out the paces, it was easier to count 1,000 for a mile than 1,200. Their decimal mile of 1,000 paces of 5ft should have been 1,200 paces of 5ft to equal a geographic mile.

1,000 paces of 2 x 36" steps would have given them the geographic mile, 100 such paces the stadium, but perhaps the 36" step was too big for them.

Their mile of 5,000 ft they divided by 8 to give a furlong of 625ft. The object here was that the furlong should have a length equal to a Greek stadium, but the problem was that their feet were too big! The stadium was 600 Greek feet but the Romans had to use the number 625 in order to be 1/8th of the new 5,000ft mile.

The answer was to reduce the size of the foot by $\frac{600}{625}$ thus giving the smaller Roman foot which is 24/25ths of the Greek foot so that 625 Roman feet equal a Greek stadium.

Of the two gentlemen with the 30" steps, one had been in the RAF, which adopted the old cavalry drill and the other had been in a tank regiment – which replaced the cavalry when it became out-dated.

By comparison, infantry units, traditionally, as well as having different 'beats' or times to the step can have different lengths of step – e.g. 33" – the length of the stick or Sumerian yard and 240 such steps of 33" (120 paces) would give the furlong of 660ft.

Readers who have been in the army may recall that the Regimental Sergeant-Major used to call out the time on every second foot, with his "left, left, left-right-left". This is why the classical pace is reckoned as two steps, because for a marching unit, it is easier to count time this way.

The pace-stick of the R.S.M. has marks for the various paces, the 33" step being the maximum. The standard step is 30" (the great cubit!) and the marching speed 120 steps to the minute. Today this step is universal throughout the Forces since standardisation of the steps helps to avoid confusion when soldiers are serving with Joint Service Units. Imagine the problems with, say, a mixed squad of soldiers and airmen, being given orders by a naval commander. Once one has been drilled into starting on the left foot, or halting on the left foot, it is not so easy to adapt to orders being given for the 'wrong' foot.

The object of all this, is that say we wished to survey and measure the length of a piece of Salisbury Plain. We could do it with tapes or chains, theodolites or even aerial photographs. The simplest method of all would be to borrow a regular soldier, wind him up, and set him pacing. At 120 steps/minute, after

> 2 minutes he would have covered a stadium,
> 20 minutes, a geographic mile and
> 1 hour, a league of three miles.

The classical tradition is that a man can march for 10 hours a day and at a pace of 60" or 2 steps a second, he would cover 10 leagues per day, or 36,000 paces in 36,000 seconds!

The English acre is traditionally the amount of land a man can plough in a day and has come to be recognised as a strip of land 66ft (1 chain) by 660ft (1 furlong).

The furlong of 660ft (600 Sumerian feet) which was 240 yards of 33" could be considered a 'long' furlong giving a 'long' acre, but the true measure of the stick was the great cubit of 30" and 240 of these measures give the true stadium of 600ft.

By comparison to the 'long' acre, the geographic acre was presumably a unit of 60ft (1 schonia) by 600ft (1 stadium). The geographic acre was consequently 36,000 sq.ft. and the 'English' acre, 36,000 sq Sumerian feet. A square stadium was therefore 10 geographic acres and the square geographic mile or minute of arc 1,000 of these acres.

The stadium when divided by 6 gives the plethrum of 100ft. This unit is today called the engineer's chain and is divided into 100 links of 1ft. The plethrum is of course 1 second of terrestrial arc, there being 360 x 60 x 60 seconds or plethra in the circumference and the plethrum can be halved, quartered or divided by 8 to provide the 'sacred' reed of 12.5ft.

The Sacred Reed is of comparable height to a modern surveying staff, with the facility of decimal or duodecimal subdivision. When incorporated into the Great Reed of 15ft, it may be seen as a particularly refined instrument – the Golden Reed, similar to our man-sized measuring stick but pivoting at the end of the sacred reed. It could thus be compared to an instrument used in map and model making known as a proportional dividers which, depending on the scale set, reduces the distance between the points at one end to the scale of the model at the other end.

The man-sized stick is thus a fifth scale of the Golden Reed. On this basis, the Angel using the Golden Reed as a pace-stick would need to be ..... a veritable giant!

After the crusade to Jerusalem, the great cathedral building epoch began. They set to, to build a house for the Lord. Not only did they utilise the sacred geometry, but look at the size of the house. He would have no difficulty moving round the aisle, amongst the great vaulted arches, or in the choir – the lowest roof at Ely cathedral is in the 16th century Lady chapel and is 60ft... four great reeds high.

GENESIS

1/26 "And God said, let us make man in our own image...."

6/1 "And it came to pass, when men began to multiply on the face of the earth, and daughters were born unto them,

2 That the sons of God saw the daughters of men that they were fair; and they took them wives of all which they chose.

3 And the Lord said, My spirit shall not always strive with man, for that he is also flesh; yet his days shall be an hundred and twenty years.

4 There were giants in the earth in those days; and also after that, when the sons of God came into the daughters of men, and they bare children unto them, the same became mighty men which were of old, men of renown.

5   And God saw that the wickedness of man was great in the earth, and that every imagination of the thoughts of his heart was only evil continually.

6   And it repented the Lord that he had made man on the earth, and it grieved him at his heart.

7   And the Lord said, I will destroy man whom I have created from the face of the earth, both man, and beast, and the creeping thing, and the fowls of the air; for it repenteth me that I have made them."

DEUTERONOMY 3/11 tells of the last of the giants.....

"For only Og king of Ba-shan remained of the remnant of the giants; behold, his bedstead was a bedstead of iron; ... nine cubits was the length thereof, and four cubits the breadth of it, after the cubit of a man."

If the cubit here referred to was the sacred cubit of 25", then the bedstead had a length of 18¾ft and the occupant a presumed height of about 18ft, ... three times that of "son of man".

We have already investigated units of measure based on distance, but now we have to consider Time as a unit of measure. We are all accustomed to a day consisting of 24 hours, of 60 minute of 60 seconds. So the second is the smallest unit of time with which we are familiar. In one second, the circumference of the Earth would have turned on its axis a quarter of a geographic mile, which is 1,000 geographic cubits or 100 great reeds. The presence of a smaller unit of time is indicated which would equal 1 great reed and be a 100th of a second. Of this unit, there would be the same number in a year of 365.2422 days as there are diametric units (half-inches) in the circumference of the earth, say 3155692597. But the smallest unit of Sumerian time was not 1 second, but 1/36,000th of a second during which period the Earth or perfect sphere would turn through 1 diametric unit of one half-inch.

The base side of the Great Pyramid was found by Cole's survey to have a length of 9069.435 inches. This is exactly 1/8th of a minute of latitude at the equator and implies a scale of 1:43200. The 43200th part of an equatorial circumference of 3155692597 diametric units (24,902.877 statute miles) is 36524.22 inches.

Smyth and Newton looked for the number 36524.22" in the pyramid as related to days in the year and assumed the number should have been in 'pyramid' inches which they adjusted from English inches. The secret of the Pyramid then could be that the English inch is equal to half a minute of equatorial degree divided by the mean length of the solar orbit expressed in days. Put another way, it also implies that the orbital period in days has been 'set' to equal half a degree of longitude at the equator!

Thus the solar year of 31556925.9747 seconds corresponds to the equatorial circumference of the Earth in diametric units of half-inches....i.e. 315569297.47 half-inches or 24,902.8 statute miles.

And even more amazing,

$$\frac{\text{circumference } 24{,}902.8 \text{ miles}}{\text{solar year } 365.24219 \times 360{,}000} = \text{foot of } 12''$$

Steccini considers all the classical units of measure to be related to the stadium of 184.8 metres with corresponding foot of 308mm. Since the length of the foot can be determined from the latitude of the observer, it follows that if one knows the value of the foot, one can work back to find the latitude of the observatory. Steccini gives the Egyptian foot as more precisely 307.7957mm which is derived from latitude 27° 30'N... Middle Egypt... and the Greek foot as 308.2764mm which is derived from 37° 30'N...Greece.

The average figure, which gives us the geographic foot of 308mm, suggests an observatory at 32° 30'N which takes us back to the latitude of BABYLON.

The ratio of 2:1 is all important both in the measures described beforehand just as it is for pursuers of the Grail, 21 being the Grail number.

The diametric unit was doubled as the inch, the hand doubled became the foot and the measuring stick could open out fully to 2 great cubits or 1 pace of 10 great or 12 sacred hands. Similarly the Sacred Reed is a half unit which opens out fully to a 'double sacred reed' of 10 great cubits or 12 sacred cubits and comes together with the 'double great reed' in a unit which contains 12 of the former and 10 of the latter – the 'half' stadium of 300ft.

Say we consider distance as the length between the two ends of a swinging pendulum.

From A – B is one unit. But from A – B and back to A could also be called one unit. The first is one diametric unit and the second is two diametric units which is one inch. As a unit of measure, both would be equally valid.

We have found that the smallest unit of distance namely the inch, is really a double unit of 2 x 1 diametrons. Similarly, it could be that the smallest unit of time is also a double unit of 2 x half-seconds. The army marches at one step per half-second which gives one pace per second or 120 steps to the minute.

Many countries count their hours as 24 in a day, but in Britain they are counted as 12... in the morning ... and 12... in the afternoon. Just like the ticking of a clock or pendulum. This is the natural rhythm of the Solar Cycle. The Earth on its orbit travels from solstice to solstice, each being half the circumference of the orbit.

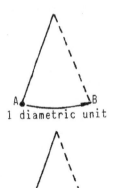

Today, we know perfectly well that a year is the time for the earth to make an orbit of the sun. But if we had to observe the cycle for ourselves, what would we see? Well, for a time, the sun would travel north, then it would turn about and head south for an equal period. In between these two 'solstices', there would be a time when day and night were equal, the equinoxes. To gauge time, we could count the whole cycle as a year, or more simply, just count the period between the solstices or equinoxes, dividing our year into a 'north year' and a 'south year'.

If the year were counted as two 'periods' from solstice to solstice or equinox to equinox, the account of Genesis 6/3, that, of man, "yet his days shall be an hundred and twenty years" would be reduced to 60 of our years ... precisely the lifespan of the average man today.

In Egypt, the solar year consisted of 360 days with an extra five, or in some cases six, days tacked on to the end as feast days. The Egyptian day was decimal, and having divided the year into 12 months of 30 days, they divided each month into 3 weeks of 10 days and each day into 10 hours of 100 minutes of 100 seconds.

The Sumerian year was also divided into 360 days, but they opted for a division of 12 'double' hours or danna of 30 ges making 360 ges for the day. Each ges was one degree of the Earth's rotation and if further divided into 60 minutes would be one minute of earth's rotation (1 geographic mile) on the Earth's surface.

The number 360 or 360 x 100 (36,000) was a favourite for subdivision and with 360 days to the year, they could choose between 10 months of 36 days comprising 6 weeks of 6 days, or 12 months of 30 days with the further choice of 6 weeks of 5 days or 5 weeks of 6 days.

When the Lord made Heaven and Earth, he did so in a period of six days, but he ought to have made the length of the year 360 days instead of the awkward 365¼ days.

The Maya of Central America had a calendar of extreme sophistication and inscribed their monuments continuously with a calendar date relative to a fixed date of origin in the past.

Unlike the Egyptians, with their year of 36 x 10 days, the Mayans used a period known as a tun of 18 x 20 kins, making 360 kins for the 'year' and adding on an extra five kins to complete the cycle.

This suited their notation which was based on the number 20 and arranged in columns not unlike the modern binary system.

alautun	kinchiltun	calabtun	pictun	baktun	katun	tun
64000000	3200000	160000	8000	400	20	1
= 20	x 20	x 20	x 20	x 20	x 20	x 1

Today, the Earth orbits the Sun at a distance of 92.95 million miles. Light travels at 186,000 statute miles per second so the orbit radius ought to have been the more perfect 93 million miles to give a mean diameter to the orbit of 186 million miles. A particle of light would then take 1,000 seconds to cross the diameter of the Earth's orbit and using this as a unit of time, an observer on the Earth's equator would turn through......

36,000,000 diametric units
1,000,000 geographic cubits or
100,000 great reeds

The geographic cubit and the great reed can be seen
as units of distance related to

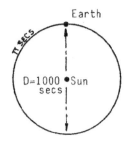

the time of the Earth's revolution and diameter of the orbit. The distance travelled by the planet on a theoretically circular orbit could also be divided by the number of days, minutes or seconds in a year to provide a unit of distance.

If we were an imaginary Babylonian orbiting the Sun at 93,000,000 miles radius or to be precise according to Funk & Wagnells Encyclopaedia covering a distance of 583,400,400 miles and dividing this great circle into 360 days, we would cover a theoretical distance of 18.756 miles in a second. This might be slightly too large a unit for everyday use, so we could divide again by 36,000 to find a yard of 33.01" – which is actually the Sumerian yard of 50 Sumerian shusi!

The famous Babylonian tower apparently had a base and a height of 3600 inches – the 'stadium' of 300ft. It was in concept a cube, although the physical building was a ziggurat or stepped tower of considerable geometric refinement. There were seven steps, each in the way of a mathematical progression, being 360 inches shorter than the one before it and ending with the base wall of 144 sacred cubits.

GENESIS 11 tells us that in the beginning.....
11/1 "And the whole earth was of one language and of one speech.

4 And they said, Go to, let us build a city and a tower, whose top may reach unto heaven; and let us make a name, lest we be scattered abroad upon the face of the whole earth.

5 And the Lord came down to see the city and the tower, which the children of men builded.

6 And the Lord said, Behold, the people is one, and they have all one language; and this they begin to do: and now nothing will be restrained from them, which they have imagined to do.

7 Go to, let us go down, and there confound their language, that they may not understand one another's speech.

8 So the Lord scattered them abroad from thence upon the face of all the earth: and they left off to build the city.

9 Therefore is the name of it called Babel; because the Lord did there confound the language of all the earth: and from thence did the lord scatter them abroad upon the face of all the earth."

The fall of Babylon is further described in the Revelation of St. John.

16/1 "And I heard a great voice out of the temple saying to the seven angels, Go your ways, and pour out the vials of the wrath of God upon the earth.

18 And there were voices, and thunders, and
    lightnings and there was a great earthquake,
    such as was not since men were upon the
    earth, so mighty an earthquake, and so great.

19 And the great city was divided into three
    parts, and the cities of the nations fell: and
    great Babylon came in remembrance before
    God, to give unto her the cup of the wine of
    the fierceness of his wrath.

20 And every island fled away, and the
    mountains were not found."

By surveying the remaining stone monuments and
circles found in Western Europe and America, the
megalithic yard has been found to have the
following values;

Britain	2.720ft	32.64"	829.0mm
Madrid	2.742ft	32.90"	835.7mm
Mexico	2.749ft	32.99"	837.9mm
Peru	2.750ft	33.00"	838.2mm
Burgos	2.766ft	33.19"	843.0mm
Texas	2.778ft	33.33"	846.7mm

(from Megalithic Sites in Britain by A.Thom,
Clarendon Press)

If the megalithic yard were carried around as a
stick, it would appear, or so it has been suggested,
that it lost its precise value through being
transported from place to place. But we should note
that the figure for Peru, 33.0", is exactly that for the
Sumerian yard i.e. 33.0", and the figure for Mexico
at 32.99" is not far off the Sumerian yard of 33.0"
either!

It could also be said that the megalithic or
Sumerian yard could co-incidentally be related to

the minute of arc. Thus the figure of 33.01" which we derived from the distance travelled by the Earth in a 36,000 part of a second using a year of 360 days could be seen as the 2200th part of a minute of latitude, giving a minute of 6051.8ft which the table of latitudes tells us would be correct for the parallel of 18° 38' South – the parallel of Lake Poopo in Bolivia which as my previous book "Atlantis: The Andes Solution" details, is the site which geographically corresponds to the location of Plato's lost city of Atlantis.

The Yard of 33.0" has been found in Sumeria as 50 shusi, in the Indus Valley as 25 Indus Valley inches, also in England, Peru and Mexico. We should be careful then not to confuse it with the megalithic yard of 2.72ft, which is a definitive unit in its own right, well documented and scientifically recorded. The origin of the megalithic yard will confirm its unique properties as intended to relate not to the figure of the globe, but to its travels through space.

Revelation 13/18 "Here is wisdom. Let him that hath understanding count the number of the beast: for it is the number of a man: and his number is Six hundred threescore and six."

666 The orbital velocity in hundreds of statute miles per hour of the planet on which man lives.

The ancient Greeks for all their powers of reason lacked one thing, the observatories and the observations. Well before their time, in France and Britain, megalithic man was aligning thousands of stones and rings and observing the positions of stars and planets for many centuries. If he had deduced the velocity of this planet on its orbit, with 365¼ days to the year he might have found it to be virtually 160,000 statute miles a day or 66600 miles per hour, which, continuing the Babylonian tradition of dividing miles per second by 36,000, would have given him the unit known as – *the megalithic yard.*.

There are in fact three different ways of measuring the length of the year, giving the Solar year of 365.24219 days, the Sidereal year of 365.25636 days and the Anomalistic year of 365.25964 days.

The sidereal year is the time taken for the Earth to return to the same point on its orbit relative to the stars and is about 20 minutes longer than the solar year, which is the time to reach the same point relative to the sun.

The sidereal year is 365 days, 6 hours, 9 minutes 11 seconds
and the solar year is 365 days, 5 hours, 48 minutes 46 seconds

The sidereal day is shorter than the solar day with 24 hours, 56 minutes and 4 seconds making 366.25 'star' days in a sidereal year.

Had megalithic man computed the distance travelled by the Earth in a 36,000th part of a second using the Solar year of 365.24219 days, then with a mean radius to the sun of 93,000,000 miles, he might have found a megalithic yard of

$$\text{circumference} = \frac{93,000,000 \text{st. m.} \times 2 \times pi \times 63360''}{365.24219 \text{days} \times 24 \text{hrs} \times 3600 \text{secs} \times 36000}$$

$$= 32.59''$$
$$= 2.71 \text{ft}$$

However, there is yet another and more interesting possibility. When the Earth's orbit has a diameter corresponding to the exact figure for the speed of light (186,282.6 miles/second from the British Astronomical Association Handbook), then by the same equation the megalithic yard would have a value of

$$\frac{\text{Speed of light}}{\text{solar year}} = \frac{186282.6 \times \text{pi} \times 63360''}{365.24219 \times 24 \times 360 \times 360}$$

$$= 32.639''$$
$$= \underline{2.719\text{ft}}$$

which is the exact figure found by Prof A. Thom for the stone circles of the British Isles.

Since the Earth on its elliptical path must of necessity cross this theoretical circle on four occasions per year to reach its maximum and minimum distances from the sun, we can say that the megalithic yard has a value directly related to the period of the orbit, the distance from the sun, and the speed of light.

We could now consider the equation complete since the Great Circle of the Earth's equator can be seen as 3155692597.47 diametric units (half-inches) and the Great Circle of the Earth's orbit as 31556925.9747 seconds (solar year). So in 1 second the Earth turns through 100 Great Reeds of 360 diametrons (half-inches) and travels on its orbit 18.5 statute miles and to sum up... in a 36,000th part of a second, the Earth's equator turns through 1 diametric unit (half-inch) and the Earth travels on its orbit through space 1 megalithic yard!

The conclusion is perhaps threefold. Firstly there is evidence that the Earth was accurately surveyed in antiquity and that this survey formed the basis of a sophisticated system of measurements.

Secondly, this system may once have been universal at a time when "the whole Earth was of one language and one speech." Or does this mean that one unknown ancient civilisation had the capability for world wide navigation and travel. Within recorded history, all the nations had a fragmented and confusing jumble of differing but related systems, similar to the further statements of Genesis, "Go to, let us go down, and there confound their language, that they may not understand one another's speech."

Thirdly, was the megalithic yard conceived to fulfil a specific function or merely as a mathematical nicety? If we are to travel through space and time, then it is unlikely to be using the elementary rocket technology prevailing today. The Holy City was seen as a Cube and "descended out of Heaven from God". It was 1.42 statute miles long on each side and should we imagine that side as enclosing a ring or circle, then we can't help thinking of the modern application for a large ring – the particle accelerator.

It has so far proved impossible to accelerate a particle beyond the speed of light for the following reason. The more the speed of the particle increases, the more its mass increases, and the more the mass increases, the more the particle slows down. Nonetheless it has proved to be the case so far that the larger the size of the ring, the closer will be the approach to the speed of light and we may wonder ultimately what will be the optimum size of the

particle accelerator? Is there some hidden secret in
Ezekiel's description of the Holy City which when
successfully decoded will enable Man to reach the
stars? Is controlled particle acceleration the way to
travel through Time?

Taking the description of St John at face value, it
does sound very much like a 'spaceship' descending
from heaven and there is no reason why it could not
have been of such an immense size with a wall of
500 reeds or 1.42 miles per side and this has
obviously inspired the cube-like spaceship featuring
in certain editions of 'Startrek'. But the text of
Revelation has to be read in conjunction with that
of Ezekiel.

And who was Ezekiel and where did he live and
when? Ezekiel is one of the Old Testament prophets
writing around 572BC at a time after Jerusalem had
been captured by King Nebuchadnezzar of Babylon
and the Jews themselves carried off to Babylon. He
tells you himself in Ezekiel 40 that his vision (and
description of the holy temple) took place "In the
five and twentieth year of our captivity" in other
words he was writing in Babylon.

So let me finally put this question... When is a
cube not a cube? Answer – when it is a ziggurat.

Mathematically speaking, a ziggurat is a cube
since its height is equal to one of the sides of its
square base, just as St John's text says...
(Revelation 21/16) "the length and the breadth and
the height of it are equal."

But physically, a ziggurat is a stepped pyramid,
each step representing a mathematical progression

and ending with a temple (the house of god) at the top.

The ziggurat at Babylon (the tower of Babel) was built in seven stages, each stage 360' or 6° lower in height than its predecessor and the width of each stage represented a parallel of latitude beginning with the 33° latitude parallel of Babylon itself (see Steccini/Thompson "Secrets of the Great Pyramid").

According to an ancient text the ziggurat had a height of 295ft and a square base which measured 295ft per side. When this was measured by modern day archaeologists they found the base to measure 300ft per side (Readers Digest – "the World's Last Mysteries"). Now a base of 300ft would be 3600 inches which in turn would be 144 sacred cubits of 25" which we will recall was the dimension of the wall given in Revelation 21/17 "And he measured the wall thereof, an hundred and forty and four cubits, according to the measure of a man, that is, of the angel."

The ziggurat in turn was surrounded by an outer wall and it seems likely that the 500 reed wall of Ezekiel which also measured 12,000 'furlongs' or great cubits in Revelations giving a side of 1.42 miles and perimeter of 5.68 miles was the perimeter wall which enclosed the grounds of the ziggurat and temple complexes. In fact, a substantial perimeter wall of exactly this dimension, 5.68 miles in perimeter has been found surrounding the temple complexes at Uruk, the ziggurats at Ur and Uruk also reaching heights of 300ft. A wall of similar dimensions also surrounded the temple complexes at Babylon and within this wall which was a triple wall

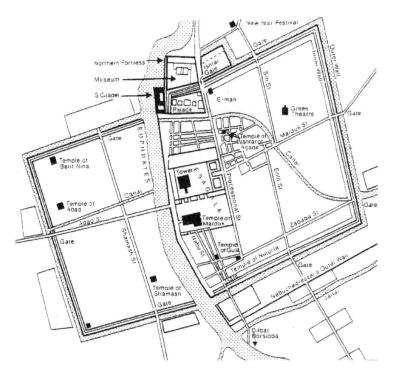

Schematic plan of the inner city of Babylon showing the temple complexes and perimeter wall (which was actually a triple wall) approximately 12,000 great cubits of 30″ in perimeter (rendered as "furlongs" in St. John) giving rise to the 500 reeds of 6 great cubits per side quoted by Ezekiel. Within the triple wall lay a further, double wall making the inner complex a square.

At the centre lies the seven-stepped ziggurat whose height and base sides measured 300ft which is the 144 sacred cubits (of 25″) quoted in the Revelation of St. John.

The house or temple of God was constructed on top of the upper, seventh step and a separate temple or House of God was also constructed outside of the innermost courtyard. The river Euphrates runs through the centre of the city.

Illustration by courtesy of "Babylon" by John Oates, pub Thames & Hudson 1979 with outer and inner gates, lay various temples with their respective courtyards, with the stepped ziggurat right at the centre again contained within its own courtyard. In Babylon, the central complex was bisected by the river Euphrates which ran through its centre, just as the city described by Ezekiel had a river which flowed out eastwards crossing through the desert to discharge into the sea.

Just as the Biblical description of the Flood has a predecessor in the Sumerian flood legends of Gilgamesh, it seems on reflection very reasonable that Ezekiel could have been given a guided tour of the ziggurat or Tower of Babel (which means 'Gateway of God') by his captor priests, and used these dimensions as the basis for the City/Temple seen in his vision.

The origins of the Sumerians themselves is not completely known, did they bring their mathematical system with them when they arrived on the Plain of Shinar or did they originate it there? That the Ziggurat should have a base side of 300ft is curious since a normal stadium of 600ft would be a 1/10th of a minute of degree but a stadium of 300 ft would be a 1/20th of a minute of degree and the number 20 was the cornerstone of Aztec or middle American mathematics. The Aztecs claimed to come from the island of 'Aztlan' which today we can identify as the island of Atlantis – presently called South America - (see my previous book "Atlantis: The Andes Solution") and readers of that book will recall that the physical dimensions of the rectangular plain Plato described as being the site of Atlantis were 3,000 x 2,000 stades.

This rectangular plain we previously identified as the Bolivian Altiplano adjacent to Lake Poopo and it measured on the ground 3,000 x 2,000 stades or "half-stades" of between 297ft to 330ft depending upon where you measure from so could nominally be described as 300ft – the unit mentioned above. Confirmation that this unit of 300ft was at one time considered to be a 'stade' is further given in a quotation by the Greek historian Herodotus who visited the Tower of Babel in 454BC twenty five years after it had been made a ruin by the conquering Persian king, Xerxes. Herodotus recorded that the site contained a "solid central tower, one furlong square with a second erected on top of it and then a third etc". Since the tower physically measures 300ft per side, then 300ft is the length of this particular 'furlong' or stadium. This confirms that Plato's stadium relative to the Plain of Atlantis was not necessarily the 600ft stadium of the time in which he was writing, but an earlier 300ft stadium such as that used in the Tower of Babel or 330ft if in "Sumerian" measures measuring the plain at its widest part and the correct physical dimensions of the rectangular plain on the Bolivian Atliplano.

The Sumerians used a measuring system based on the shusi of 0.66", with a foot of 20 shusi = 13.2", cubit of 30 shusi = 19.8", yard of 50 shusi = 33" and double yard of 66" which is 100 shusi.

Some ancient units were related in the ratio of 24/25 for example the Roman foot was 24/25ths of the Greek geographic foot.

If we apply this formula to the Sumerian cubit of 19.8", then 25/24ths of the Sumerian cubit is 20.625" which is virtually the Egyptian "profane" or "royal" cubit and would give a corresponding "remen" of 14.584" which when multiplied by 5,000 to the minute of arc gives a minute of arc of 6076.69ft (compare to today's figure of 6076.8884ft)

The prime numbers of Sumerian mathematics were 12, 24, 60, 360, 36,000 etc.

It seems curious that the Babylonians who counted in shusi of 0.66" should build a ziggurat with a side which is a multiple of inches or half-inches instead of shusi. And given their knowledge of the Earth's diameter and Earth based units, why should they continue to measure in shusi?

If we look at the Earth's equator in terms not of miles or inches, but in the diameter based half-inches then the Equator (24,901.55miles) when divided by the solar year gives a unit of:

$$\frac{24{,}901.55 \text{miles} \times 63{,}360" \times 2}{365.24219 \times 24 \times 60 \times 60} = 100 \text{ units of half-inch}$$

Again, why didn't the ancient Sumerians use the Earth based half-inch unit?

The Sacred and Great cubits were "pure" units directly related to the size of the Earth and also related to the daily Earth's rotation, but the Megalithic Yard was an attempt to reconcile an Earth based unit with a Time based unit.

When we look at the actual speed at which the Earth travels through space on its direction towards the constellation of Hercules, we find that it has a speed of approximately 12.5 miles per second.

This might have given an ancient astronomer an equation like this;

12.5 miles x 63360"
   = 792000inches
   = 1,000 surveying chains of 1200
                                                  shusi
   = 12,000 double yards of 100 shusi
   = 24,000 yards of 50 shusi
   = 40,000 cubits of 30 shusi
   =100,000 links of 12 shusi

And again, the speed at which the Milky Way galaxy as a whole moves towards the constellation of Leo is about 375 miles per second (Funk & Wagnalls Encyclopaedia) which gives:

375 miles x 63360"
            = 23760000inches = 36,000,000
                                            shusi
            or

      1,000 shusi in a 36,000th part of a
                  second.

It would seem that the ancient Sumerians or their predecessors rejected an Earth-based unit in favour of a space-based or astronomical unit!

J. Alden Mason writing in "The Ancient Civilisation of Peru" quotes measurements of lines set out on the plain of Nazca which have standard lengths of 595ft – in Babylonian/Sumerian units this would suggest a standard length of 360 Sumerian cubits of 19.8″ was intended.

He also quotes roads in Peru as being of a standard width of 33ft – and 33ft is half a standard surveying chain from Babylon/Sumeria and comprises 50 links each of 12 'shusi' of 0.66″ or 60 hands each of 10 shusi of 0.66″ which either way comes to 20 Sumerian cubits of 19.8″.

The distance between rest houses on the royal Inca roads he tells us was a standard of 4½ miles – which in Sumerian units would be 360 standard surveying chains of 66ft (each chain was 60 feet in length if we use the Sumerian foot of 13.2″ which was 20 Sumerian shusi).

As to Inca bricks, Alden Mason gives the average size as being 32 by 8 by 8 inches – in units of Sumerian shusi of 0.66″ this would suggest a brick of 48 x 12 x 12 shusi was intended.

It would seem therefore to present clear evidence for a Sumerian presence in South America and the question must be, did the Sumerians sail there, or given the other point of view – did the Sumerians themselves originate in South America?

Appendix A

Since this book was originally written back around 1980, great advances have been made in portable computers, Internet technology which makes information freely available and in particular, the free distribution of satellite imaging with Google Earth.

This has made possible the analysis of ancient plots and field systems in Mexico and Bolivia which confirm the existence of "Sumerian" and "Egyptian" cubits and measuring units in those countries in pre-Columbian times.

In Tabasco, Mexico, can be seen square regular plots set out in units of 10 x "stades" of 165ft i.e.1650 x 1650 feet which would be 10 x 100 "Sumerian" cubits per side.

On the Altiplano in Bolivia, not far from La Paz, can be seen remains of square plots set out in "stades" of double the above measure, i.e. "stades" of 330ft making them 330ft x 330ft or 200 x 200 "Sumerian" cubits. This turns out to be the size of plot Plato described when he said the rectangular plain of Atlantis measured 3,000 x 2,000 stades and it is in fact a double unit of the other "Atlantean" (or "Sumerian") stade of 165ft or 100 cubits.

The stade of 100 cubits provides the root for many of the other measurements units both in "Egyptian" cubits and in "Sumerian" cubits since whether a unit is "Sumerian" or "Egyptian" simply depends on whether you divide the square plot of 165 ft in halves, quarters, thirds etc. for example the 165ft plot can be divided by 100 to give "Sumerian" cubits or by 96 to give "Egyptian" cubits, by 48 to give "Mayan hunabs", by 60 to give Sumerian yards etc

The city of Teotihuacan and other Mexican monuments such as El Castillo in Yukatan are similarly set out in "Sumerian" feet and cubits as can be determined not only from Google Earth measurements, but from a correct analysis of measurements taken on site by previous researchers and even including modern high tech laser surveys such as in the case of El Castillo.

The calendar of Tiwanaku in Bolivia was based upon a row of 11 standing stones which divided the year into 20 "months" of 18 days with the extra days dispersed at the ends when the sun "stood still". It also incorporated a lunar calendar based upon 2 x 20 sidereal lunar months so that every three years the solar and lunar calendars meshed together, not only that but every three years it also synchronised with the Synodic lunar calendar (based upon the phases of the moon) when an extra month was added to the synodic lunar calendar so that 37 synodic lunar months equalled 40 sidereal lunar months equalled three solar years.

Every 30 solar years an extra month had to be added to the lunar calendars to bring them back into synchronisation with the solar calendar, and all this information is preserved in the number of icons called "chasquis" shown on the nearby Gate of the Sun.

The width of the Tiwanku calendar was intended to be 96 Sumerian cubits, and the perimeter of a theoretical circle which would enclose it and relate to the year would have a diameter of 2 x 96

Sumerian cubits and a perimeter of 360 Sumerian yards of 50 shusi, marking out in Sumerian yards the 360 day year and at the same time the perimeter would be 365.24 "Megalithic" yards marking out the actual year.

CONCEPT
The Circle of the Earth

Circumference	Radius	Diameter
360 degrees of	10,000,000	1,000,000,000 diametric units comprising
60 miles of	sacred	10,000 miles of
12,000 hands of	cubits	10,000 hands of
12 diametric units	of 25"	10 diametric units

10 diametric units = 5" sacred hand
12 diametric units = 6" great hand
20 diametric units = 10" sacred foot
24 diametric units = 12" English foot
50 diametric units = 25" sacred cubit
60 diametric units = 30" great cubit
100 diametric units = 50" double sacred cubit
120 diametric units = 60" pace of 2 gt. cubits

The circle = 360 degrees
degree = 360,000ft
Great Schonia = 36,000ft
League = 18,000ft
Mile = 6,000ft
Stadium = 600ft
Short Stade = 300ft
Plethrum = 100ft
Schonia = 60ft
Reed = 15fr
Decapode = 10ft
Fathom = 6ft
Pace = 5ft
Ell = 4ft
Yard = 3ft
Foot = 1ft = 2 hands = 4 palms = 12 inches = 16 fingers = 24 diametric units
1 hand = 2 palms = 6 inches = 8 fingers = 12 diametric units
1 palm = 3 inches = 4 fingers = 6 diametric units
2 inches .... = 4 diametric units
1 inch .... = 2 diametric units
1 diametric unit

60 inches pace = 120 diametric units
30 inches great cubit = 60 diametric units
25 inches sacred cubit = 50 diametric units

The Sumerian Units

10 shusi	= 1 Sumerian hand	of	6.60"
12 shusi	= 1 Sumerian link	of	7.92"
20 shusi	= 1 Sumerian foot	of	13.20"
24 shusi	= 1 double link	of	15.84"
30 shusi	= 1 Sumerian cubit	of	19.80"
50 shusi	= 1 Sumerian yard	of	33.00"
100 shusi	= 1 double yard	of	66.00"
360 shusi	= 1 gar		

Order of the Cubits

Great Cubit	= 30 inches
Sacred Cubit	= 25 inches
Royal Cubit	= 21 inches

........rolls out

1 French toise of 6.39ft
rolls our 29ft x 30 = 1 stadium

1 Russian arshin of 7ft
rolls out 22ft x 30 = 1 furlong

The Stadium

1200 great hands of 12 diametric units (half inches)
600 feet of 12"
400 geog cubits of 18"
240 great cubits of 30"
120 paces of 5ft
600ft x 60ft
36,000 sq ft
5 Sumerian feet

The Furlong

1200 Sumerian hands of 10 shusi
600 Sumerian feet of 20 shusi
400 Sumerian cubits of 30 shusi
240 Sumerian yards of 50 shusi
= 600 x 60 Sumerian feet
43,560 sq ft..... 120 wheels of

The English Furlong

660ft x 66ft

40 Poles of 16.5f...........	=	40 poles of 15 Sumerian feet
10 chains of 66ft...........		= 10 chains of 60 Sumerian feet
1 furlong of 660ft...........		= 1 furlong of 600 Sumerian feet

40 great reeds of 15ft
10 schonia of 60ft
1 stadium of 600ft

English Acre

.... = 36,000 sq Sumerian feet

4,840 sq yds...........

Sumerian Acre

= 16,000 sq Sumerian cubits

Geographic Acre

.... = 16,000 sq geog cubits

16,000 sq geog cubits

213

Values of the Units
1 English inch = 25.399772mm taken as 25.4mm

Foot

English	12.0"	304.8mm	derived from polar diameter
Saxon	13.2"	335.3mm	20 Sumerian shusi
Roman 1	13.18"	335.0mm	similar to Saxon foot
Roman 2	11.65"	295.9mm	24/25ths of the Greek foot
Paris 1	12.785"	324.74mm	1/6th of toise diameter of wheel
Paris 2	12.789"	324.84mm	diameter of wheel
Russian	14.0"	355.6mm	diameter of wheel
Greek	12.136"	308.3mm	Greece latitude
Babylon	12.126"	308.0mm	Babylon latitude and Phoenicia
Egypt 1	12.118"	307.8mm	Egypt latitude
Egypt 2	11.81"	300.0mm	circumference as pi 3141592653
Remen	14.58"	370.3mm	mean of latitudes

Cubit

Egypt 1	18.177"	461.7mm	Egypt latitude
Egypt 2	17.716"	450.0mm	circumference as pi 3141592653
Royal 1	20.62"	523.7mm	circumference of earth in atur
Royal 2	20.6264"	523.9mm	diameter of earth in atur
Royal 3	20.669"	525.0mm	circumference as pi 3141592653
Royal 4	20.72"	526.3mm	circumference as 40,000,000mtrs
Sumerian	19.8"	502.9mm	24/25ths of Egyptian Royal cubit
Greek	18.205"	462.4mm	Greece latitude
Babylon	18.1889"	462.0mm	Babylon latitude and Phoenicia
Tiwanaku	20.0" (508mm) or 20.17" (512.3mm)		latitude of Tiwanaku

Megalithic Yard

Britain	2.72ft	32.64"	829.0mm	year of 365¼ days
Sumeria	2.750ft	33.0"	838.2mm	year of 360 days
India	2.750ft	33.0"	838.2mm	year of 360 days
Peru	2.750ft	33.0"	838.2mm	year of 360 days

Statute Mile 5280ft or 8 furlongs of 240 Sumerian yards

Geographic Mile

	6076.8884ft	mean of meridians latitude
	6056.97ft	Egypt middle latitude
	6062.99ft	Babylon latitude
	6068.46ft	Greece latitude
	6046.3418ft	equatorial latitude
	6087.268ft	equatorial longitude
	6107.7755ft	polar latitude
Nautical mile	6080.00ft	Admiralty sea mile

Relationship of Sumerian and Egyptian cubits to stade of 165 feet.

English Feet of 12"	Stade	20 shusi — Sumerian Feet of 13.2"	30 shusi — Sumerian cubits of 19.8"	50 shusi — Sumerian yards of 33"	12 shusi — Sumerian links of 7.92"	1 shusi — Sumerian Shusi of 0.66"	Sumerian poles of 16.5ft	Egyptian Cubits of 20.625"
33	1/5th	30	20	12	50	600	2	
41.25	1/4		25	15		750		24
55	1/3rd	50		20	100	1000		32
66	2/5ths	60	40	24		1200	4	
82.5	½		50	30	125	1500	5	48
99	3/5ths	90	60	36	150	1800	6	
110	2/3rds	100		40		2000		64
165	1	150	100	60	250	3000	10	96
198		180	120	72	300	3600	12	
220	1+1/3	200		80		4000		128
264		240	160	96	400	4800		
297		270	180	108	450	5400		
330	2	300	200	120	500	6000	20	192
396		360	240	144	600	7200	24	
440		400		160		8000		256
495	3	450	300	180	750	9000	30	288
528		480	320	192	800	9600	32	
660	4	600	400	240	1000	12000	40	384
792		720	480	288		14400	48	
825	5	750	500	300	1250	15000	50	480
990	6	900	600	360	1500	18000	60	576

215

Plot of 100 × 100 "Sumerian" cubits of 19.8"cubits

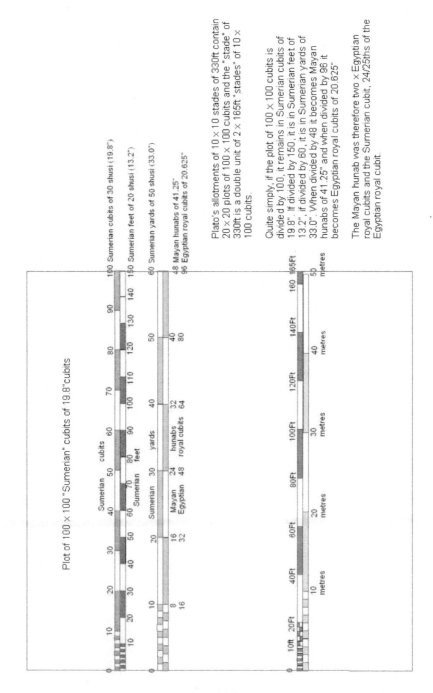

100 Sumerian cubits of 30 shusi (19.8")
150 Sumerian feet of 20 shusi (13.2")
60 Sumerian yards of 50 shusi (33.0')
48 Mayan hunabs of 41.25"
96 Egyptian royal cubits of 20.625"

Plato's allotments of 10 × 10 stades of 330ft contain 20 × 20 plots of 100 × 100 cubits and the "stade" of 330ft is a double unit of 2 × 165ft "stades" of 10 × 100 cubits.

Quite simply, if the plot of 100 × 100 cubits is divided by 100, it remains in Sumerian cubits of 19.8". If divided by 150, it is in Sumerian feet of 13.2", if divided by 60, it is in Sumerian yards of 33.0". When divided by 48 it becomes Mayan hunabs of 41.25" and when divided by 96 it becomes Egyptian royal cubits of 20.625".

The Mayan hunab was therefore two × Egyptian royal cubits and the Sumerian cubit, 24/25ths of the Egyptian royal cubit.

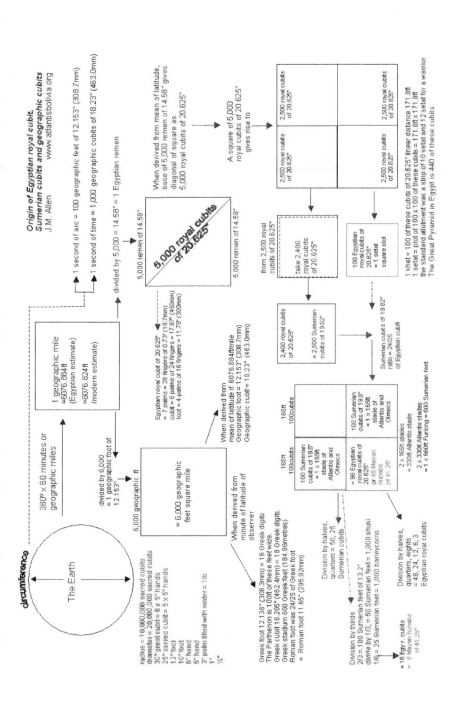

Origin of Egyptian royal cubit,
Sumerian cubits and geographic cubits
J.M. Allen   www.atlantisbolivia.org

circumference

The Earth

radius = 10,000,000 sacred cubits
diameter = 20,000,000 sacred cubits
30" great cubit = 6 x 5"hands
25" sacred cubit = 5 x 5" hands
12"foot
10"foot
6" hand
3" palm filled with water = 1lb
1"
½"

360° x 60 minutes or
geographic miles

divided by 6,000
= 1 geographic foot of
12.153"

6,000 geographic ft

= 6,000 geographic
feet square mile

1 geographic mile
=6076.884ft
(Egyptian estimate)
=6076.624ft
(modern estimate)

1 second of arc = 100 geographic feet of 12.153" (308.7mm)

1 second of time = 1,000 geographic cubits of 18.23" (463.0mm)

divided by 5,000 = 14.58" = 1 Egyptian remen

When derived from mean of latitude,
base of 5,000 remen of 14.58" gives
diagonal of square as
5,000 royal cubits of 20.625"

5,000 remen of 14.58"

5,000 royal cubits
of 20.625"

5,000 remen of 14.58"

A square of 5,000
royal cubits of 20.625"
gives rise to

2,500 royal cubits of 20.625"	2,500 royal cubits of 20.625"
2,500 royal cubits of 20.625"	2,500 royal cubits of 20.625"

When derived from
mean of latitude if 6076.884ft/mile
Geographic foot = 12.153" (308.7mm)
Geographic cubit = 18.23" (463.0mm)

Egyptian royal cubit of 20.625"
= 7 palms = 28 fingers of 0.73" (18.7mm)
cubit = 6 palms of 24 fingers = 17.67" (450mm)
foot = 4 palms of 16 fingers = 11.78" (300mm)

When derived from
minute of latitude of
observer

from 2,500 royal
cubits of 20.625"

take 2,400
royal cubits
of 20.625"

100 Egyptian
royal cubits of
20.625"
= 1 setat
square plot

2,400 royal cubits
of 20.625"

= 2,500 Sumerian
cubits of 19.82"

Sumerian cubits of 19.82"
Sumerian cubits of 19.82"
ratio = 24/25
of Egyptian cubit

1 khet = 100 of these cubits of 20.625" linear distance 171.8ft
1 setat = plot of 100 x 100 of these cubits = 171.8ft x 171.8ft
the standard allotment was a strip of 10 setat and 12 setat for a warrior
The Great Pyramid in Egypt is 440 of these cubits

Greek foot 12.136" (308.3mm) = 16 Greek digits
The Parthenon is 100ft of these feet wide.
Greek cubit 18.205" (462.4mm) = 18 Greek digits
Greek stadium 600 Greek feet (184.98metres)
Roman foot was 24/25 of Greek foot
= Roman foot 11.65" (295.92mm)

165ft 100cubits	165ft 100cubits
100 Sumerian cubits of 19.8" stade of Atlantis and Olmecs	100 Sumerian cubits of 19.8" stade of Atlantis and Olmecs
= 96 Egyptian royal cubits of 20.625" = 48 Mayan hunabs of 41.25"	2 x 165ft stades = 330ft Atlantis stade 2 x 330ft Atlantis stades = 1 x 660ft Furlong = 600 Sumerian feet

Division by halves,
quarters = 50, 25
Sumerian cubits

Division by thirds
2/3 = 100 Sumerian feet of 13.2"
divide by 1/3, = 50 Sumerian feet = 1,000 shusi
1/6, = 25 Sumerian feet = 1,000 barleycorns

Division by halves,
quarters, eights
= 48, 24, 12, 6, 3
Egyptian royal cubits

=16 Egyr. cubits
= 8 Mayan hunabs
of 41.25"

Printed in Great Britain
by Amazon

19888363R10129